History's Most
Rogues
and Villains

History's Most Daring
Rogues
and Villains
Dirty Rotten Scoundrels

Nigel Blundell

PEN & SWORD
TRUE CRIME

First published in Great Britain in 2022 by
PEN AND SWORD TRUE CRIME
An imprint of
Pen & Sword Books Ltd
Yorkshire – Philadelphia

ISBN 978 1 39901 767 1

A CIP catalogue record for this book is available from the British Library.

Typeset in Times New Roman 10.5/13 by
SJmagic DESIGN SERVICES, India.
Printed and bound in the UK by CPI Group (UK) Ltd.

Pen & Sword Books Limited incorporates the imprints of Atlas, Archaeology,
Aviation, Discovery, Family History, Fiction, History, Maritime, Military, Military
Classics, Politics, Select, Transport, True Crime, Air World, Frontline Publishing,
Leo Cooper, Remember When, Seaforth Publishing, The Praetorian Press,
Wharncliffe Local History, Wharncliffe Transport, Wharncliffe True Crime and
White Owl.

For a complete list of Pen & Sword titles please contact
PEN & SWORD BOOKS LIMITED
47 Church Street, Barnsley, South Yorkshire, S70 2AS, England
E-mail: enquiries@pen-and-sword.co.uk
Website: www.pen-and-sword.co.uk

Or
PEN AND SWORD BOOKS
1950 Lawrence Rd, Havertown, PA 19083, USA
E-mail: Uspen-and-sword@casematepublishers.com
Website: www.penandswordbooks.com

Contents

Introduction

There are powerful motives for those who roam onto the wrong side of the law. Greed is the most usual. Ambition is another. Lust sometimes plays a compelling part. But many illicit acts are committed for no other reason than a driving sense of adventure.

These various motives link the disparate bunch of characters in this book. Gathered together within these pages is a roguish array of artful tricksters, fantastic fakers, rascally fraudsters and cunning conmen.

Most fall into that last category, and it was a small-time American conman named William Thompson who was responsible for the term. After gaining the trust of his target, the trickster would ask: 'Have you confidence in me to lend me your watch?' When the victim did, Thompson vanished. On his arrest in 1849, the *New York Herald* dubbed him 'the confidence man' and the name stuck. His adventures may have inspired Herman Melville's 1857 novel *The Confidence-Man* – plus, it would seem, two centuries of con-artistry, spanning the time range of this book.

Ever since, this type of scam has been thought of as a raffish crime, spawning scores of anti-heroes in books, movies and TV series. They tend to be judged not so much by what they do but the style in which they do it. As author Robert Louis Stevenson said: 'The Devil, depend upon it, can sometimes do a very gentlemanly thing.' However, the characters gathered together here have, contrary to appearances, all proved themselves less than gentlemen or ladies.

Many fall into the category of outright villains. Yet the irony is that however reprehensible their deeds, these scoundrels often display the very essence of enterprise and adventure. It would be wrong to condone their antics, of course, but it is difficult not to admire their artifice.

If, as the saying goes, 'the Devil has the best tunes', he certainly also has some of the best stories – and here are some of the most startling of recent times. Together they're the diabolically fiendish work of *History's Most Daring Rogues and Villains*.

Eddie Chapman
The Cool Spy Codenamed 'Zigzag'

No writer of fiction could have made up the story of Eddie Chapman; it would have been too unbelievable. A womaniser, wastrel, army deserter, petty thief, pickpocket, confidence trickster, fraudster, forger, burglar and safe blower, Chapman was also a master of espionage who became a hero to both British intelligence and Germany's Nazi leaders during the height of the Second World War. And unlike many cases of conmen whose exploits are self-embellished, the personal history of this flamboyant philanderer has been firmly proven as fact.

Edward Chapman, son of a publican, was born in 1914 in the ancient English village of Burnopfield, originally the site of a fourteenth-century leper colony, near Newcastle upon Tyne. At the age of 17, in search of adventure, he joined the Army but within a year was locked up for going absent without leave. On his release, he was dishonourably discharged and made a beeline for London's seedy Soho district where he worked as a barman, a wrestler, a dancer and a movie extra. When those failed to adequately fund his love of low women and high living, he embarked on a career of crime.

Graduating from petty theft, Chapman became a forger – earning him a two-month jail sentence – then a house breaker and finally a safe breaker. He joined a ruthless bunch of criminals called the 'Jelly (gelignite) Gang', who used explosives to break into the safes of upmarket London stores. Among the estimated fifty raids they carried out over two years, they made off with £15,000 from a pawnbroker and several mink coats from a furrier. So proud was he of his handiwork that Chapman cut out newspaper reports of his exploits and kept them in a scrapbook.

It was not only safes he broke but women's hearts. 'He attracted women on the fringe of London society,' according to a later MI5 interrogation report, 'indulged in violent affairs and then proceeded to blackmail them by producing compromising pictures.'

Scotland Yard began dogging the gang's footsteps, so in 1939 the Jelly Gang switched operations to Scotland where Chapman and three others were caught red handed breaking into an office building in Edinburgh. Awaiting trial, however, the 25-year-old crook fled to the Channel Islands where he was joined by his latest girlfriend Betty Farmer. She later recalled: 'I was 22 and in love with the most handsome and charismatic man I had ever seen. I couldn't remember being happier.'

During a carefree Sunday lunch with her at Jersey's Hotel de la Plage, he spotted an undercover policeman pretending to be a fellow guest and, rather than risk arrest, leapt from his seat, kissed Betty on the shoulder and dived through the restaurant window in a shattering shower of glass. That same night, the inveterate crook attempted another bungled burglary, was caught and given a two-year prison sentence on the island, with an extra year being added for an escape attempt, after which he would be returned to the mainland to face a far longer jail term. Fate then intervened in the most extraordinary way – to his undeserving advantage.

In July 1940 the Germans, having conquered most of Europe, occupied the Channel Islands in preparation for their planned invasion of Britain. Eddie Chapman was now a prisoner of the Nazis – though not for long because in October 1941 he was freed on parole along with a jailbird friend, 22-year-old Anthony Faramus. Together they went into business as barbers, mainly serving German military clients, although their shop was little more than a 'front' for a black market racket in illicit and stolen goods. Keen to get off the island, the pair wrote to the German authorities offering their services as spies. Referring later to this treasonable suggestion, Chapman noted: 'I thought that if I could work a bluff with the Germans, I could probably be sent over to Britain.'

It didn't work out quite as planned. Chapman and Faramus were arrested on suspicion of plotting espionage – not for but against the Third Reich. The pair were transported to the Nazi prison and transit camp of Fort Romainville on the outskirts of Paris for what threatened to be a dangerous grilling. There, with his skill at breaking and entering, Chapman purloined a pass key to the women's quarters and spent romantic interludes with the female prisoners, mainly French and Belgian, before slipping back past the sleeping guards in the morning.

Finally, he was handed over to the German military intelligence service, the Abwehr, in whose custody the glib-tongued prisoner won a reprieve. His interrogators saw merit in their captive's criminal skills and offered him not only his freedom but a healthy pay package as a fully-fledged spy. While Faramus was left behind in jail, ending up in a concentration camp but surviving the war, Chapman was sent to La Bretonnière-la-Claye, a 'school for spies' near Nantes. There, under the direction of top Abwehr spymaster Baron Stephan von Gröning, he was trained in explosives, radio communications, unarmed combat, parachute jumping and other clandestine arts in preparation for being dispatched to Britain to commit acts of sabotage. At the end of the course, he was given the code name Fritzchen (Little Fritz).

Alongside the training sessions, Chapman enjoyed a luxurious lifestyle. The spy school was housed in a beautiful chateau where he enjoyed fine food, wine and cigars. He later wrote of his astonishment at the credulity of the Abwehr officers who seemed less interested in evaluating information than in enjoying the high life on French soil, fiddling their expenses and supplementing their service pay with currency rackets. Eventually, however, Chapman's training was put to use and he was briefed on his first mission.

On 16 December 1942, Chapman was put aboard a Focke-Wulf bomber and flown to Britain. Equipped with £1,000 in used fivers, a radio transmitter, pistol, invisible ink and a cyanide pill, he parachuted out over the Cambridgeshire countryside, where he found a telephone kiosk (other reports say he knocked on the door of a farmhouse), rang the police and turned himself in. Handed over to MI5 secret service agents, Chapman related his extraordinary story and immediately offered to become a double agent. In truth, he had little choice; with his criminal record he could otherwise be facing many years in jail. In addition, MI5 already knew of Little Fritz's existence: having decrypted German radio codes, they had already arrested and 'turned' several German spies under the so-called Operation Double-Cross.

Chapman was taken to Latchmere House, a mansion west of London otherwise known as Camp 20, where many captured agents were housed. There he revealed to his interrogators the ambitious mission contracted to him by his German spymasters: the blowing up of the De Havilland aircraft factory at Hatfield, Hertfordshire, where the RAF's revolutionary new twin-engine Mosquito fighter-bomber was being built. And as far as the Germans knew, that is exactly what he did.

A fake explosion was enacted at the plant on the night of 29 January 1943 and subsequently reported in the press. To substantiate the supposed act of sabotage, a team of stage designers from London's Old Vic theatre draped a huge canvas painted like ruins over the factory's main transformer building. Papier-mâché dummies were laid amid shattered concrete and broken furniture. The mocked-up 'damage' was later confirmed by Luftwaffe reconnaissance. Chapman did his part by sending a wireless report to his German handler von Gröning, who sent back a congratulatory message.

The Nazis' rogue spy Little Fritz was now known by the British as Agent Zigzag, in acknowledgement of his erratic loyalties. Yet he was not universally considered a hero. One of his case officers, Major Michael Ryde, complained of a 'disreputable' reliance on drink and prostitutes, demanding that 'the Zigzag case must be closed down at the earliest possible moment.' However, his superior, Lieutenant Colonel Robin Stephens, won the argument, saying

'Chapman should be used to the fullest extent. He genuinely means to work for the British against the Germans. By his courage and resourcefulness, he is ideally fitted to be an agent.'

Chapman, still in his twenties, certainly showed courage. According to National Archives documents revealed half a century later, he offered to blow up Adolf Hitler with a suicide bomb. He told his Camp 20 handlers that German spymaster von Gröning had promised that if the British mission was successful he would take him to a Nazi rally, where his reward would be to be placed 'in the first or second row' close to Hitler's podium. Chapman said: 'I believe he will keep his promise. Then I will assassinate Hitler. With my knowledge of explosives and incendiary material, it should be possible.' A startled MI5 officer, Ronnie Reed, responded: 'Whether or not you succeeded, you would be liquidated immediately.' To which Chapman retorted: 'Ah, but what a way out.'

The offer was not taken up but MI5 set about capitalising on their double-agent's skills in other ways, having him voluntarily return to Europe to again pander to his Nazi masters. In March 1943, masquerading as a steward, Chapman sailed on a merchant vessel to neutral Portugal, where he jumped ship and reported to the German Embassy in Lisbon. There was one further obstacle to overcome. His German minders had wanted him to blow up the vessel with two carefully placed bombs disguised as lumps of coal. MI5 couldn't allow a British ship to be blown up, yet did not want to compromise their double agent, so devised an elaborate plot to make the Abwehr believe it would explode after leaving Lisbon.

Returned to Germany for debriefing, Chapman was feted as a hero. He was given a military pass identifying him as an *Oberleutnant*, born to German parents in New York, and a Reich passport in the name of Fritz Graumann. Armed with these papers, he was flown to occupied Norway to teach at a Nazi spy school in Oslo – effectively a nine-month holiday as a reward for his mission to Britain. While there, he secretly photographed his fellow spies to provide future evidence against the officer relishing the spoils, but for most of the time enjoyed the privileged life of a German officer enjoying the spoils of Nazi conquest. By now a genuine friend, von Gröning joined his top spy in Norway and handed him the equivalent of £15,000 as a reward for being the agent who had 'showed the most outstanding zeal and success during the year.' He also conferred an even more astonishing tribute – making his pal Eddie the only British citizen ever to be awarded Germany's highest military honour, the Iron Cross.

It was early 1944 before British intelligence heard of Zigzag's whereabouts. MI5 officer Sir John Masterman, who chaired the Double-Cross Committee in charge of 'turning' German spies, wrote: 'News trickled through of a mysterious figure in Oslo speaking bad German in a loud voice, wearing a checked suit and given full reign of a private yacht. From those details alone, we thought it must be Zigzag.'

As if life was not already heady enough, Chapman was drinking at The Ritz in Oslo when he met and fell in love with a 20-year-old Norwegian girl, Dagmar Lahlum, to whom he eventually confided that he was not a Nazi officer but a British agent. This delighted Dagmar because she was already in contact with the Norwegian resistance, and they worked together to gather information against the invaders. 'We had a great love match,' he later said, 'and I had the intention of going back and marrying her.' When he was sent on his next mission, he neglected his promise and she assumed him dead.

Her double-dealing fiancé was, of course, very much alive. After D-Day in 1944, Chapman was parachuted back into Britain to report on the accuracy of Germany's V-1 flying bombs, which were dropping from the skies over central London and causing severe damage both to buildings and civilian morale. At the behest of MI5, he sent back misleading reports that the V-1s were overshooting their urban targets. The result was that the Germans 'corrected' their range so that many fell short of the capital and landed in rural Kent, thereby doing far less damage and saving many lives. As far as the Nazis were concerned, it was another successful mission for Little Fritz.

Eddie Chapman survived the rest of the war living a life of relative luxury in London. His Norwegian lover Dagmar did not fare as well. Despite his promise, he did not return to marry her. In fact, the double agent's faithlessness was doubly ungallant because while wooing Dagmar he already had a fiancée in London, stage dancer Freda Stevenson. Tragically, in newly liberated Norway, Dagmar was wrongly accused of being a Nazi collaborator. Believing Chapman to be dead and thereby unable to prove that he had been a British agent, she was convicted of consorting with him and jailed for six months.

Chapman abandoned both women after the war and instead tried to track down his former lover Betty Farmer, whom he had left in a hurry at Jersey's Hotel de la Plage in 1939. He later wrote: 'Uppermost in my mind was the desire to find Betty, my girl whom I had last seen when I dived through a hotel window.' To help in the hunt, he engaged private detectives and briefed them over lunch at London's swanky Berkeley Hotel. One of them, wondering what they should be looking for, asked him: 'Is there anyone here who resembles her?' Chapman pointed to a blonde at the far end of the crowded dining room. 'That girl looks like her from the back,' he said. When she turned slightly, he added: 'Jesus! It is Betty!' Strolling over to her, Chapman tapped her on the shoulder – and, having believed him dead, all that the shocked Betty could manage to say was: 'Where did you spring from?'

Betty's errant lover proposed and, although she delayed saying 'Yes', they married in 1947. 'I knew I wasn't going to have anything like a normal married life but with him life was exciting,' she said. 'Eddie once said it was better to live one day as a tiger than a whole life as a lamb.' In 1954 Betty gave birth to a daughter, Suzanne. When she married, the best man was her father's old friend Baron von Gröning.

Chapman published an account of his exploits in three books: *The Eddie Chapman Story* (1953), *Free Agent: The Further Adventures of Eddie Chapman* (1955) and *The Real Eddie Chapman Story* (1966). A film based on his life, *Triple Cross*, was released in 1966. His story was also told in two books published in 2007, *Zigzag – The Incredible Wartime Exploits of Double Agent Eddie Chapman* by Nicholas Booth, and *Agent Zigzag: The True Wartime Story of Eddie Chapman, Lover, Betrayer, Hero, Spy*, by Ben Macintyre. Betty Chapman later told her own story in *Mrs Zigzag* (2013).

The full account of the exploits of one of Britain's most valuable spies was revealed only when MI5's files on him were released to The National Archives in 2001. Their charismatic subject would have revelled in his renewed notoriety. Aged 83, Eddie Chapman died, with devoted Betty at his side, on 11 December 1997.

MI5 officer Sir John Masterman once wrote of Chapman: 'In fiction, his story would be rejected as improbable. The subject is a crook but, as a crook, he is by no means a failure. Of fear he knows nothing. Adventure to Chapman is the breath of life. Given adventure, he has courage to achieve the unbelievable.'

Phineas T. Barnum
Fortune from Freaks and Frauds

The Hollywood musical *The Greatest Showman* portrayed its title character, Phineas T. Barnum, as a dazzling visionary whose inventive genius conceived what we now know as 'showbusiness'. He also originated big-top circus extravaganzas, launched the first superstar tour with singer Jenny 'the Swedish Nightingale' Lind and is considered the father of modern advertising because of his remarkable talent for grabbing the attention of the public. Finally, with the fortune he had made as the world's most famous impresario, he reinvented himself as a philanthropist, reforming politician and anti-slavery campaigner.

All very commendable, as portrayed in the 2017 epic by actor Hugh Jackman, who described Barnum as 'the man who ushered in modern-day America'. Except it wasn't quite like that...

In truth, Phineas Taylor Barnum built an ill-gained fortune on freaks and fraud. The movie airbrushed out the showman's mistreatment of his circus animals and his cynical exploitation of some of America's most vulnerable misfits. His most famous attraction, 'General' Tom Thumb, was employed at the age of five and made to act as an adult by smoking cigars and drinking alcohol. Even more disturbing was his characterisation of his African-American 'exhibits', some of whom were displayed in cages as 'wild men' and one of whom, billed as 'George Washington's 160-year-old nanny', he had purchased as a slave. He is credited with coining the phrases 'Never give a sucker an even break' and 'There's a sucker born every minute' – and he lived his entire life by following these two adages.

Strangely, there was an early portent of the character that this garrulous trickster would become. How fitting that when Barnum was born on 5 July 1810, his austere Puritan parents should name the child Phineas, a Biblical title that in Hebrew means 'Brazen Mouth'. Through his early years growing up in Bethel, Connecticut, however, big-mouth Barnum had an uphill struggle to achieve his ambitions. A discontented Jack of all trades, Phineas was a store clerk, ran lotteries, sold men's hats, edited a newspaper, sold a fire extinguisher that couldn't put out a fire, took orders for a cargo ship that never carried a cargo, and was joint owner of a grocery store. Despite this modest success, he saw himself as a failure and was determined to become an entrepreneur at any cost.

In the first real surge of his adventurous spirit, he sold his interest in the grocery business and embarked on a bizarre adventure into showmanship. He had learned the most elementary lessons while working in a barter store in Bethel. Here, goods were paid for not in cash but in kind. Because so much suspect merchandise was being offered, the store's policy was always to offer faulty goods in return. As Barnum recalled: 'Everything in that store was different from what was represented.' Burnt peas, for instance, were offered as coffee beans and cotton in place of wool.

With this insight into fair trading, 25-year-old Phineas, now married to Charity Hallett and the father of two children, took his family to New York and opened a Broadway sideshow. His first exhibit was an ugly and withered black lady named Joice Heth whom he had come across in a similar sideshow in Philadelphia. Poor Joice, blind and partly paralysed, claimed that she was 160 years old and had once been George Washington's nursemaid. Barnum bought her on the spot for a pittance. Then he plastered Manhattan with posters:

> The greatest curiosity in the world and the most interesting, particularly to Americans, is now exhibiting at the saloon fronting on Broadway; Joice Heth, nurse to General George Washington, the father of our country, who has arrived at the astonishing age of 161 years, as authentic documents will prove, and in full possession of her mental faculties. She is cheerful and healthy though she weighs but 49 pounds. She relates many anecdotes of her younger master.

Displaying his great flare for publicity, Barnum dreamed up incredible tales for the press and learned the lesson that free editorial space is much more cost-effective than expensive advertising. So astute was Barnum that he even wrote anonymous letters to the newspapers calling into question the claims about Joice. He reasoned that it was better to have people talking about you than not and, as many confidence tricksters have reaffirmed since, bad publicity is better than no publicity. Crowds queued along the sidewalks of Broadway to see the 'female Methuselah'. And they certainly got their money's worth with her phoney memories of Washington, the many errors in her narratives being excused because of her extreme antiquity.

When initial interest in his 'Methuselah' died down, Barnum took an advertisement in a newspaper to announce that Joice Heth was not a real person at all but a robot. The crowds flocked back when he proclaimed: 'What purports to be a remarkable old woman is simply a curiously constructed automaton, made up of whalebone, india-rubber and countless springs ingeniously put together and made to move at the slightest touch.'

Long after she retired through ill health, Barnum took great care of her. On her death in 1836, however, he found a new way of making money out of her. He hired a surgeon to perform an autopsy on Joice in front of an invited audience. Barnum had long known that she was nothing like her advertised age but he roared with laughter when it was revealed that the old lady had fooled even him. The surgeon pronounced Joice to be no more than 80 years of age. 'I, like you, have been duped,' said the irrepressible Barnum, and his name remained in the news for another few weeks.

Joice Heth had not been Barnum's only exhibit, of course. There was his 'Feejee Mermaid' which he claimed had been fished out of the Pacific in 1817. In fact it was, in Barnum's own words, 'an ugly, dried-up, black-looking and diminutive specimen' which he had bought from a Boston showman in 1842. He kept his acquisition secret at first while he distributed 10,000 leaflets arguing that mermaids existed and displaying engravings of beautiful specimens disporting themselves on rocks. No mention was made of Barnum's own ugly specimen until, public interest having been awakened, he announced its arrival at the museum. Thousands of people handed over their ten cents to see what was nothing more than a monkey's torso attached by amateurish taxidermy to the tail of a large fish.

The manner in which he presented some of his human exhibits was even more indefensible. Dreadlocked black males were displayed in cages as 'Wild Men of Africa'. Another African-American boy, William Henry Johnson, suffered from microcephaly, giving him a tiny, sloping head. Labelled 'Man Monkey Zip the Pinhead', he was dressed in fur and 'performed' by shrieking and rattling the bars of his cage. Other attractions included Jo-Jo, the 'dog-faced boy' who had to bark for his living, bearded lady Annie Jones whose facial hair grew down to her breasts, 'Lionel the Lion Man' who had extra hair glued on his face, and Isaac Sprague the 'Living Skeleton' who suffered from muscular atrophy, at 5ft 6in tall but weighing only 44lb.

Other acquisitions included black conjoined twins Millie and Christine and black brothers Eko and Iko, all of whom had originally been kidnapped from their parents as children for their 'freak show' value. More famous, however, were Chang and Eng Bunker, billed as 'The Siamese Double Boys', who were joined at the chest. The pair were astonishing acrobats and were glad to work for Barnum as they earned a small fortune. Although they bickered constantly, they married two sisters and are reputed to have fathered twenty-one children between them before dying within three hours of each other in their early sixties.

There were even more blatant frauds. Barnum persuaded spectators to pay to view 'the horse with its tail where its head should be' – only to encounter an ordinary horse tethered in its stall back to front, with its tail in the feeding trough. Barnum even exhibited an ordinary black alley cat, advertising it as 'the world's only cherry coloured cat'. When his customers complained, they were told that the animal was the colour of black cherries!

Richer from displaying Joice Heth and his other fraudulent acts, Barnum took to the road in the late 1830s with the country's first canvas-top circus. However, when the love of his family drew him back to New York, he found the showbusiness game tougher than ever. A string of short, theatrical ventures led him finally to a 'go for broke' gamble. Scudder's American Museum was up for sale, a five-storey shell of a building that had been a money loser for years. With nothing for collateral but his dreams, Barnum convinced the owners that he could ride their white elephant into fields of glory. And he did. From the date of its opening on 1 January 1842, Barnum's American Museum was destined to become the new wonder of the Western World. He displayed educated dogs and jumping fleas, fat boys and giants, dwarfs and rope dancers, performing 'Indians' and the first Punch and Judy Show ever seen in New York.

Being Barnum, however, the virtues of every act were wildly exaggerated. The fleas were advertised as 'insects that can draw carriages and carts' and it was only when the punters had paid their money that they discovered that the conveyances were suitably minuscule. At the other end of the scale, a live hippopotamus was also exhibited in the American Museum. It would have been a big enough draw in its own right but Barnum could not resist billing it as 'the great behemoth of the Scriptures'.

In three years, Barnum paid for his museum and expanded it beyond even his wildest dreams. With his incredible imagination and sense of the bizarre, he entertained millions. Still seeking fresh phenomena to tempt, tantalise and astonish audiences, the super-showman then made a find that would turn out to be one of his greatest: tiny Tom Thumb. Barnum's half-brother, Philo, tipped him off that a remarkable midget was being exhibited at Bridgeport, Connecticut. Barnum dropped everything, raced north and examined him. He discovered a bright, 5-year-old boy of amazingly minute proportions. The child had been born on 4 January 1838 weighing nine pounds and had developed normally until the age of six months. Since then, however, he had not grown another inch and, due to dwarfism, stood at just 25 inches high. Barnum signed up the little fellow on the spot for $3 a week.

The youngster was called Charles Stratton. With his showman's flair, Barnum renamed him General Tom Thumb and made him his prime attraction. Not content with the truth, Barnum billed the child as 'a dwarf of 11 years of age just arrived from England'. He taught him to act 'autocratic, impudent and regal' and dressed him in various guises, from a mini-Cupid to a Roman gladiator to Napoleon Bonaparte. The partnership between the 6ft showman and tiny Tom was a remarkable one which developed into an enduring friendship. As Tom Thumb grew into adulthood, he remained a perfectly formed midget, 2ft tall and weighing 15lb. What he lacked in size, the brilliant little man made up for in personality. With patter, songs and dances devised by Barnum, he made theatrical history – and enough money to ensure his and Barnum's passport to even greater fame abroad.

There were overflow crowds when Tom Thumb and his supporting cast appeared at a London theatre, and a command performance was given at Buckingham Palace, where even Queen Victoria was amused. There were audiences with King Louis Philippe of France, Queen Isabella of Spain, Belgium's King Leopold and other European royals. With sell-out performances and with gifts from the crowned heads, the three-year European tour made Thumb and Barnum very rich. Their association would continue for thirty years, and it was the warm-hearted midget who came to Barnum's aid when fate dealt the entrepreneur a flurry of blows.

Back in the United States, in 1850 Barnum met opera star Jenny Lind, the 'Swedish Nightingale' and sponsored her on an American tour which was a forerunner of the modern rock roadshow, earning them millions in fees and merchandise. But in 1855 disaster befell him. Always a soft touch for his friends, to whom he was devoted and loyal, Barnum had underwritten a dying enterprise, the Jerome Clock Company. When his friends plummeted into bankruptcy, they took Barnum with them. The next blow was the burning down of Barnum's home, 'Iranistan'. The palatial mansion and international showplace exploded into flames after a painter dropped a lit cigarette.

The greatest blow, however, came in 1865 when Barnum's precious American Museum was also destroyed by fire. Wild animals escaped onto the streets of New York, an orangutan being recaptured in an office block. A gallant fireman single-handedly carried the 400lb Fat Lady to safety but the 7ft 11in World's Tallest Woman had to be lifted free with the aid of a derrick. It all made huge headlines; Barnum saw to that. No one was killed in the museum blaze but the loss of the half-a-million cherished exhibits was heartbreaking for Barnum. The damage was put at $500,000 but the insurance covered only a fraction. He faced ruin. At this point Tom Thumb stepped in and revealed himself as big of heart as he was small of frame. He helped finance a new European tour which was the beginning of Barnum's second fortune. By 1870 he had repaid his creditors, rebuilt his museum and opened his newest, bigger, better-than-ever circus.

When Barnum formed a partnership with James Anthony Bailey in 1871, the Barnum & Bailey Circus reached its zenith with the three-ring spectacle that became circus tradition. 'The Greatest Show On Earth' travelled across North America in its own railroad cars, adding new words and phrases to the English language, such as jumbo, ballyhoo and white elephant.

Barnum's white elephant was called 'Toung Taloung' and had to be repainted every time it rained. More enduring, however, was a mighty elephant which Barnum purchased from London Zoo in 1882 and inspirationally renamed 'Jumbo'. The animal was advertised as 'the only mastodon on Earth, whose like the world will never see again – a feature crushing all attempts at fraud.' Thereafter the creature gave its name to everything from jumbo-sized burgers to jumbo jets. On one occasion, Jumbo seemingly felt so overworked that he embarked on a sit-down strike. Unwilling to leave England, the pachyderm refused to enter his van until Barnum bribed him with a barrel of beer. Jumbo died in 1885 after being hit by a train during a tour of Canada.

Meanwhile, Barnum's beloved wife Charity had become an invalid and died in 1873 after a series of strokes. Sick with loneliness, he took a new wife ten months later: a lovely young English girl named Nancy Fish. Barnum was 64 and Nancy forty years younger but she remained a devoted wife and friend until his own death at the age of 81.

When it became evident that his demise was close, the *New York Evening News* did a remarkable thing. With Barnum's permission, they published his obituary in advance so that the showman could read it. 'Great And Only Barnum,' the headline said. 'He Wanted To Read His Obituary And Here It Is!' Laughing, Phineas and Nancy read it together, and it was close to his bedside when the 'Great And Only' died. He left a then-massive $5million fortune – firmly proving Barnum's own adage: 'There's a sucker born every minute.'

Jim Bakker and Jimmy Swaggart
Ungodly Gospellers

Two thousand years ago, the Christian Evangelist Saint Matthew recorded a couple of top tips for those who might follow. He quoted Jesus as saying: 'Blessed are the meek for they shall inherit the Earth.' Later in his Gospel, he added the warning from Christ: 'I say to you, it is easier for a camel to go through the eye of a needle than for a rich man to enter the Kingdom of God.'

Evangelists of modern times, however, have often neglected to follow those teachings – none more so than Jim Bakker, a self-appointed holy man with some pretty unholy habits. The glitzy TV preacher also seemed to have disregarded the Biblical warning: 'The Lord giveth and the Lord taketh away.' So the hot gospeller must have got quite a shock when the Lord, having giveth him far too much, eventually had to taketh it ALL away!

Throughout the 1980s boom in 'televangelism' in America, Bakker reached the very top of his vocation by a tear-stained style of Bible-thumping which had the viewers sending in untold millions of dollars. Peak earning time was the *Jim and Tammy Bakker Show*, an extraordinary double act of syrupy sweetness and light with his blonde, bronzed, mascara-daubed wife. Born James Orsen Bakker in Muskegon, Michigan, on 2 January 1940, Bakker had married Tamara Faye LaValley in 1961 while they were Bible students at North Central University in Minneapolis. Ordained in 1964, he set off with Tammy on the path to glory by working at the Christian Broadcasting Network, hosting a daily children's show called *Come On Over* which was an immediate success.

In 1972 they went the way of so many showbusiness hopefuls by moving to California to head up an organisation called PTL. It stood for *Praise The Lord* – but it also spelt easy money for the schmaltzy TV twosome. Two years later, the Bakkers relocated to Charlotte, North Carolina, and began their own show, *The PTL Club*, which was a phenomenal success, picked up by almost 100 stations with an average viewing figure of more than twelve million. At the height of their ministry, the Bakkers were watched by thirteen-and-a-half million people across America.

What he lacked in stature Jim Bakker made up for in evangelical charisma. He preached and he appealed and, of course, the money rolled in. By the early 1980s, Jim and Tammy had built a theme park with shopping mall and hotel at Fort Mills, South Carolina. Officially described as a 'Christian-themed retreat and gospel park', others dubbed it 'Christian Disneyland'. With the grandiose title Heritage USA, the 2,300-acre park attracted six million visitors a year and briefly became the third most successful park in America, at one point grossing $130million annually. They also had a satellite system which distributed their network twenty-four hours a day across 1,200 channels. Contributions from the Bakkers' devoted followers were estimated at more than $1million a week.

If anyone criticised the televangelical bandwagon, Bakker would respond: 'I believe that if Jesus were alive today he would be on TV.' In fact, if Jesus were alive, he certainly would not have approved, particularly because the hot gospeller hid a shameful secret from his generous flock. In 1980, Bakker had taken a church secretary, Jessica Hahn, to a hotel in Clearwater Beach, Florida, where he allegedly drugged and had sex with her: according to Jessica, he pinned her down for an hour, repeatedly telling her: 'By helping the shepherd, you are helping the sheep.' He then said a short prayer before returning to the pulpit to admonish his flock for not following God's ways. It was a one-night stand that remained secret for seven years until revealed in March 1987. At the same time, Tammy Bakker's on-off dependency on drugs also came to light.

When the scandals broke, Jim Bakker denied that he had forced himself on Miss Hahn but did admit to meeting her in the hotel room. However, he claimed that he was the victim of a 'diabolical plot' to oust him from his seat of power and alleged that he had been 'wickedly manipulated' for the benefit of 'treacherous former friends'. This was a thinly veiled hint that his television rival, Jimmy Swaggart, was jealous of his supreme position as America's Number One TV evangelist. Indeed, Swaggart had recently unleashed fire and brimstone against him over the Jessica Hahn incident and, when interviewed on the *Larry King Show*, had called him a 'cancer in the body of Christ'.

Jim Bakker resigned in order to fight these irreligious slurs, leaving colleague Jerry Falwell to run PTL as a caretaker until he and Tammy were able to return to take their rightful place. Falwell was made of sterner stuff, however. He dug into PTL's dealings and discovered a black hole of funds being sucked into the Bakkers' personal accounts. It was also revealed that the pair, who travelled in 'his and hers' Rolls Royces, owned a vast Florida condominium, complete with $60,000 gold fixtures, which the preacher had described as a 'parsonage'. There was also the question of more than a quarter of a million dollars paid into an account to which Miss Hahn had access; it sounded very much like hush money.

While Jim and Tammy Bakker were off the air, supposedly marshalling their defence against these scurrilous allegations, they appealed to Jerry Falwell for a subsistence allowance. Falwell was astonished at their 'shopping list' of demands: $300,000 a year for him, $100,000 for her, a lakeside home in South Carolina, fees for attorneys, wages for security guards and a maid, plus further luxurious perks. 'I don't see any repentance there,' said Falwell. 'I see greed, the self-centredness, the avarice that brought them down.' He publicly decried Bakker as a liar, embezzler, sexual deviant and 'the greatest scab and cancer on the face of Christianity in 2,000 years of church history'.

At Bakker's fraud trial, it was revealed that money raised to spread the good word had been spread extra thinly to allow the phoney prophet to syphon off almost $5million, along with a $279,000 pay-off for Jessica Hahn's silence. Bakker, who seemingly made all the financial decisions for his organisation, kept two sets of books to conceal the accounting irregularities.

He and his attorney, the Reverend Richard Dortch, were defrocked from the PTL church in May 1987. The ensuing scandal went into overdrive, as Hahn posed nude for *Playboy* magazine before becoming a saucy chat-line DJ, while Bakker became the subject of a government inquiry into his fundraising gimmicks.

Retribution was slow in coming but in August 1989 Dortch, having agreed to testify against Bakker, was jailed for eight years. Bakker himself, after a series of tearful but self-serving TV appearances, appeared in court in Charlotte to hear his defence lawyer assure the judge that his client was 'a man of love, compassion and character who cares for his fellow man.' The judge was unimpressed and, after a five-week trial, Bakker was found guilty on all counts. He was sentenced to a $500,000 fine and forty-five years in jail. For once at least, the tears that flowed down his cheeks were perhaps warranted.

In early 1991, a federal appeals court upheld Bakker's conviction on the fraud and conspiracy charges but voided his forty-five-year sentence, together with the $500,000 fine. A new jail term was set at eight years and he was granted parole in 1995 after serving just five.

Jim and Tammy Bakker divorced in 1992. She went on to marry his best friend, Roe Messner, and died in 2007. Bakker married again in 1998, to Lori Beth Graham. He moved to Branson, Missouri, where he returned to the evangelism business, broadcasting a new daily *Jim Bakker Show*. In a supposedly confessional book, *I Was Wrong*, he admitted that the first time he had read the Bible all the way through had been in prison. He wrote: 'I was appalled that I could have been so wrong and I was deeply grateful that God had not struck me dead as a false prophet!'

Only in America could religious leaders like Bakker attain the celebrity status of TV stars. And few others raised themselves so high – in their own estimation, if not the Lord's – than his rival TV evangelist Jimmy Swaggart. If lightning were to strike twice, this was the occasion that it could reasonably have been construed as an act of heavenly judgement. For Swaggart, the preacher whom the corrupt Bakker had first blamed for his downfall, was doomed to suffer a similar fate, his disgrace being equally scandalous.

Swaggart was a braggart, boasting that, unlike Bakker, he was incorruptible. Most of his flock believed him – until they heard what he got up to in a New Orleans motel room. The evidence was in the form of photographs handed to officials from his Assemblies of God church showing Swaggart taking a prostitute, Debra Murphee, into the hotel.

Swaggart's downfall was sweet revenge for yet another TV rival evangelist, Martin Gorman, who had also been defrocked after Swaggart accused him of 'immoral dalliances' in 1986. Gorman, who ran a successful TV show from New Orleans, had launched an unsuccessful $90million lawsuit against Swaggart for spreading false rumours. In revenge, he had hired a private detective to follow his persecutor. He discovered that Debra Murphee was regularly employed by Swaggart to perform sex acts while he watched from the comfort of an armchair. Murphee went along with the lucrative sex games eventually deciding to go public with her story. She recreated Swaggart's favourite poses for *Penthouse* magazine, and the sixteen pages of explicit pictures were deemed so hot that they had to be sealed in each issue. Murphee also went on a national media tour to publicise her revelations.

Swaggart resigned from his ministry in 1988. With his long-suffering wife Frances at his side, he sobbed in front of a congregation of 7,000 in Baton Rouge, Louisiana, and confessed to 'moral failure', adding: 'I do not plan in any way to whitewash my sin or call it a mistake.' Turning to Frances, he said: 'I have sinned against you and I beg your forgiveness.'

It could have been the end for Swaggart, who had been introduced to religious fanaticism at an early age by his Pentecostal evangelist parents, Sun and Minnie Belle. Born on 15 March 1935 in Ferriday, Louisiana, Jimmy Lee Swaggart was as precocious as his cousin, the rock and roll phenomenon Jerry Lee Lewis. Jimmy sang and preached on street corners and led congregations when he was only 9 years old. He married when he was just 17 and went on the road as a full-time travelling preacher. In the 1960s he recorded gospel music albums while building up another audience via Christian-themed radio stations. In the 1970s he switched to television with *The Jimmy Swaggart Telecast* which, at its height, was broadcast on 300 channels in the US and repeated in more than 100 other countries. By the mid-1980s he had become America's most popular TV preacher.

On the face of it, the singing evangelist had not put a foot wrong in life until he fell for the charms of Debra Murphee. Because of such perfectly understandable 'moral sins', Swaggart's local church, the compassionate Louisiana Assemblies of God, was inclined to deal with him leniently and recommended a minimal three-month suspension from preaching. The national church was hardly much tougher and ordered him banished from the pulpit for a full year. Swaggart, however, unwisely defied the ban after only a few months, on the grounds that his absence would destroy his $140 million-a-year worldwide ministries. He was immediately defrocked by the Assemblies of God.

Murphee faded from the scene after a proposed movie deal about her meetings with the preacher failed to come to fruition. Swaggart, meanwhile, saw his television empire dwindle from tens of millions of viewers to mere thousands. The self-appointed mouthpiece of the Lord was merciful towards himself, telling his congregation that God had forgiven him for his sins, adding piously: 'What's past is past.'

In 1991 Swaggart was stopped by a police officer in Indio, California, for driving his car erratically – and was discovered to be sharing it with a prostitute and a pile of porn magazines. His companion, Rosemary Garcia, said Swaggart had stopped to proposition her as she stood at the roadside. She later told reporters: 'He asked me for sex. I mean, that's why he stopped me. That's what I do. I'm a prostitute.' This time, rather than confessing to his congregation, Swaggart brazened it out with the rebuff: 'The Lord told me it's flat none of your business.'

Frank Abagnale
Escapades of a High-Flying Fake

Arch confidence trickster or Walter Mitty fantasist – or, indeed, a bit of both? In the case of Frank Abagnale, no one is quite sure. His reported escapades are so amazing that a major Hollywood movie was made to tell his story – one billed as 'more fantastic than anything Hollywood could make up'. But therein lies a mystery, because no one can be sure whether the successful biopic *Catch Me If You Can* is just too fantastic to be entirely true. After all, the amiable Abagnale is one of the most resourceful weavers of fantasy of any trickster in recent history.

When dealing with the life of Frank Abagnale, it is almost impossible to separate fact from fiction. The only certainties surround the early years in the life of this flawed genius. Born in 1948 into an affluent family who ran a stationery shop in the New York suburb of Bronxville, his parents became young Frank's first victim when the 15-year-old misused their gas station credit card to buy motor parts that he could sell for a wad of dollars to impress girlfriends. The fraud was discovered only when the credit card company asked Abagnale Sr why he had bought fourteen sets of tyres and twenty-two batteries in three months.

Frank was sent to a private reform school but it had little effect and, within a year, he had moved back to New York City where he learned the art of 'paperhanging': cashing cheques issued on empty bank accounts. The only problem was that bank tellers asked too many questions of a 16-year-old, so he set about creating a new identity for himself. An airline pilot, seen as a glamorous profession in the 1960s, was, he correctly judged, the perfect guise.

Not for Frank the normal years of study and training, of course. The teenager 'aged' a few years by prematurely dying his hair grey, then he rang Pan Am pretending to be a pilot whose uniform had been stolen and asked where to get a spare one at short notice. The airline directed him to the Well-Built Uniform Company, where he was fitted out in the blue suit of a first officer – all on Pan Am's account. Then, using logos taken from a model aeroplane kit, he forged a staff ID card. The fraudster was suddenly a Pan Am 'co-pilot'.

At first, Abagnale tentatively tested his fake identity by signing into hotels used by aircrew, charging his room and all expenses to the airlines. He socialised with airline staff and dated attractive stewardesses. The hotels also cashed personal cheques for crew and Abagnale took full advantage of this.

Then the conman took to the skies. Airlines allowed each other's staff to travel free, a perk known as 'deadheading', and this often placed 'co-pilot' Abagnale in the jump seat at the back of the cockpit. On several occasions, the real crew invited him to take over the controls, putting thousands of lives briefly in his hands. The first time this happened was on a Pan Am flight between Paris and Rome when, with the aircraft cruising at 30,000ft, the captain left the cockpit to mingle with passengers in the first-class compartment while Abagnale, the very image of the confident aviator, slid into his seat. Frank was just 17 and had never flown a plane before.

Almost as audacious was the stunt he pulled when he conned Pan Am into putting him in touch with a group of school leavers who had applied to be stewardesses – and hired eight of them, all Arizona university students, to travel around Europe with him dressed as Pan Am crew. He told them it was part of a promotional tour but he was using them to boost his credibility, allowing him to cash ever-larger phoney cheques.

Abagnale got away with this double life for two years, jetting around the world, staying in luxury hotels and wining, dining and bedding hundreds of women along the way. His aerial spree ended with a close call when he was quizzed by a suspicious FBI man at Miami Airport and, although the conman talked his way out of trouble, he decided it was time for a career change.

According to the fraudster himself, by the time he was 21, he had worked as a doctor, a lawyer and a university professor, while conning banks, airlines and hotels out of $2.5million, the equivalent of around $40million today. Abagnale says he once used a forged medical certificate to convince a hospital in Georgia that he was a senior paediatrician. When asked for a diagnosis, he would always quiz a trainee doctor, then nod sagely and say: 'I concur.' He got away with this for nearly a year, only stopping when he was asked to give emergency treatment to a sick baby, finally realising he was out of his depth.

Again he moved on, working as an attorney in Atlanta before using forged papers to become a professor of sociology at a university in Utah. Abagnale boasted that by reading one chapter ahead of his students, he was able to add his own wisdom to a subject and that he was so convincing the university considered offering him a permanent post.

The FBI finally caught up with him after he had returned to his pilot's role. When an ex-girlfriend tipped off police, he was arrested in Paris and extradited to the US. But, slippery to the last, he escaped from the aircraft at New York by removing the toilet and lowering himself through the hole onto the runway.

He evaded capture yet again when two FBI agents confronted him on a street in Washington DC – by persuading them that he too was an undercover FBI man.

A month later, the conman fell for the oldest trick in the police manual. When two detectives spotted him strolling down a New York street, they called out his name and he made the mistake of looking back. He was sentenced to twelve years for his crimes but was offered parole after only four on condition that he advised the FBI how to deal with the sort of crime he had committed himself. Shortly after his release, he met his wife Kelly, whom he described as his salvation, and with whom he had three children.

As a 53-year-old ex-jailbird, Abagnale again hit the jackpot in 2003 with the release of the $40million Steven Spielberg screen adaptation of his book, *Catch Me If You Can*, with Leonardo DiCaprio playing the conman and Tom Hanks the FBI officer chasing him. 'The true story of a real fake,' was how the film was billed. 'Every scam he pulls in the movie is what he pulled in real life,' Spielberg vowed at the launch. 'There's an awful lot of authenticity in it,' added Hanks, with DiCaprio repeating the assurance that the plot was 'more fantastic than anything Hollywood could make up'. However, that did not prevent cynics alleging that a lot of Abagnale's life story had been made up – by Frank himself.

So, was *Catch Me If You Can* all truth or partly fiction? Was Abagnale both fraudster and fantasist?

Critics pointed to Abagnale's three appearances on the Johnny Carson *Tonight Show* in the 1970s, in which he confessed to an extraordinary bank robbery that netted him thousands of dollars. He told Carson that he had placed an 'Out of Order' sign on the First National City Bank of Boston's night deposit box at Logan International Airport while standing nearby in a guard's uniform with a portable box to collect the day's takings from airline and shop staff. But journalists who investigated his claims found that the bank didn't exist, and a spokesman for the similar sounding First National Bank of Boston told them: 'It never happened at our bank, never happened in Boston and never happened to the only bank that has a night deposit box out there.'

Another Abagnale boast was that he taught sociology students at Brigham Young University in Provo, Utah, after convincing his employers he was a professor. But sociology professor Barry Johnson, who taught at the prestigious college, said: 'It's news to me. To even be considered for a position at the university you must have ecclesiastical references. Without them, you just aren't going to get in.' Another of the major confidence tricks in Abagnale's life story had him spending a year as 'Dr Frank Williams' at Cobb County General Hospital near Atlanta, Georgia, where he claimed to have headed a staff of seven interns and forty nurses. However, administrators said they had no record of any Dr Frank Williams.

When Abagnale was questioned about his stories, he said: 'I impersonated a doctor for a few days, I was a lawyer for a few days. People have asked me to prove it but, due to the embarrassment involved, I doubt if anyone would confirm the information.'

Whatever parts of Frank Abagnale's story are truth and whatever fiction, the arch confidence trickster has done well out of his criminal career. Although he received only a modest sum for the film rights to his book, the silver-haired smooth talker who was once America's most wanted conman ended a career of fraud and reinvented himself as a millionaire businessman, advising companies on white-collar crime.

Anthony Williams
The Lowly 'Laird of Tomintoul'

Fraud Squad detectives would normally have celebrated the arrest of a criminal as crafty as Anthony Williams. Had he been anyone else, they would have welcomed the attention, the glory, the headlines that arose from this high-profile case. Instead, the fraudbusters of London's Metropolitan Police could only bury their heads in their hands in shocked disbelief. For the villain they had nabbed was one of their own. Anthony Williams was deputy director of finance – at Scotland Yard.

Over twelve years of lies, deception, embezzlement and downright theft, Williams had filtered away £5million of funds that should have been spent on the Yard's undercover operations. He had used it to finance a secret life, which had him opening bank accounts around the world, living as a nobleman, 'owning' virtually an entire Scottish village and being recognised as a man of considerable substance and property just about everywhere else.

There may have been some who envied or even admired one of the twentieth-century's cheekiest swindlers but others, such as Sir Paul Condon, the Metropolitan Police Commissioner, were left to pick up the pieces of the biggest, most humiliating inside job ever. At a press conference, Sir Paul offered the people of London an 'unreserved apology', admitting he was 'angry and embarrassed that the courageous work of police officers had been betrayed.' The unprecedented apology was the end of an incredible and intriguing trail of corruption leading to 55-year-old Williams's sentence of seven-and-a-half years' imprisonment on 19 May 1995.

The astonishing catalogue of deceit had begun with one small theft of £200 in 1981. The cash was earmarked as payment for an officer to take his seriously ill wife on holiday but the excuse was fictitious and the £200 was pocketed by Williams. Having succeeded so easily in his first attempt at crime, the mild-mannered accountant stole again and again – and kept on stealing right under the noses of Britain's nucleus of top crimebusters. He was in a convenient position to make his thefts easy for he was overseer of the Met's staff welfare fund, from which he began to make regular 'withdrawals'.

Just once, Williams got close to being caught. A colleague noticed that one sum didn't quite add up. Williams quickly paid in a cheque to cover the discrepancy. In total, the bespectacled, respected handler of police welfare funds siphoned off £7,000, money which should have gone to the hard up and the ill. Much of the loot was used to ease Williams's own money problems caused by the ending of his first marriage, £500-a-month maintenance payments for his two daughters and a hefty overdraft.

Over the years, Williams became proud of his deception. His bravado grew as an accountant who could not only cook the books but make them boil. Without really knowing where he could get his hands on unlimited money, Williams opened an account at Coutts, bankers to the Queen and to the uppercrust. His creation of an 'uncle in Norway' who was set to leave him a healthy inheritance not only smoothed the way with Coutts (the bank authorised a £30,000 overdraft) but was to later prove invaluable when questions were raised about his high-living ways.

In 1986, Williams was to strike gold. As deputy finance director, Scotland Yard could find no one better to handle police affairs of a highly confidential and sensitive nature. Williams was put in charge of a 'secret fund' to fight organised crime. The fund was supposedly to pay police informers and for general undercover work but only part of it was allocated for this purpose. In fact, for over eight years Williams administered two companies operating an anti-terrorist surveillance aircraft based at a Surrey airfield.

Throughout the period when he was financing the running of the plane, IRA mainland bombing was at its peak and police needed an aircraft to keep watch on suspected arms caches and 'safe houses'. So secret was the project that just a handful of people within Scotland Yard knew of the operation and Williams's involvement in it. Enquiries by any curious outsider would reveal only the existence of two firms, one apparently owned by the other, running a small, fixed-wing aeroplane.

Such was the determination by anti-terrorist squads to control the IRA's activities that the Cessna plane was in constant use. For instance, in 1989 it was used in a successful operation leading to the capture of two IRA activists at an arms dump on a desolate beach on the Pembrokeshire coast of South Wales. They were caught after a seven-week stake out, codenamed Operation Pebble. It suited Williams greatly that the plane was so heavily used. Such victories against IRA terrorists meant few worries were raised over the Cessna's costs – £250,000 in the first year alone – allowing Williams to rob the fund blind.

Whatever the Cessna operation required, Williams paid immediately. No complaints were made about his speedy requisitioning of anything from aviation fuel to paperclips. What was to come to light when Williams eventually stood trial, however, was that over eight years he requisitioned £7million – with only around £2million actually being spent. The Old Bailey court was told: 'The defendant was allowed unlimited private access on his own discretion to the funds of the Receiver, as the Yard's financial controller was known. It was placed in a specified account. He did not have to answer to anyone. He controlled the payments in and the payments out.'

As the money rolled in, Williams was glad that he had his 'uncle' in Norway to explain away such untold wealth. The inheritance story fended off questions about his grand homes and lavish lifestyle. And Williams certainly knew how to splash the cash around. The money was spread across banks and building societies in Scotland, London and the Channel Islands. He even paid cash for some of the many properties he acquired; an apartment being bought directly from the secret Scotland Yard fund. In 1989 alone, he stole more than £1million.

It was remarkable that Williams's wife Kay happily accepted the 'Norwegian uncle' story to explain the couple's elevation into a style of living most people could only dream of. It was even more remarkable that no one at Scotland Yard got wind of the millionaire lifestyle of the £42,000-a-year accountant. He brought homes in Leatherhead and Haslemere, in Surrey, and a flat in London's Westminster. He rented another flat in Mayfair which cost him £2,000 a month.

Friends he entertained lavishly marvelled at Williams's good fortune in having a foreign relative who had left him such wealth. Yet another house in New Malden, Surrey, was purchased for £178,000 cash. A holiday villa on Spain's Costa del Sol was added to the property empire. As well as Coutts, where he was given a gold bank card, Williams opened accounts at National Westminster, Standard Chartered and Clydesdale banks and the Leeds and Bradford & Bingley building societies. But it was in Scotland where Williams's stolen wealth allowed him to feel as if he owned the world.

He had fallen in love with a Highland beauty spot where he had spent several happy holidays. Tomintoul, which takes its name from the Gaelic 'Tom an t-Sabhail' ('Hillock of the Barn') was a sleepy Grampian village of 320 people, and in 1989 he decided to buy a large chunk of it. Appearing at weekends, turned out in country tweeds or sometimes a kilt, Williams first purchased a modest £6,000 cottage in The Square, on which he carried out £40,000 renovations. Then there was the £120,000 Gordon Arms Hotel, which underwent a £1.5million restoration, the old fire station (£21,000) and the Manse in Glenlivet (£192,000). Williams even had the cheek to apply to the Moray Enterprise Board for a Business Expansion Scheme grant for one of his companies, Tomintoul Enterprises, which in turn provided £3million towards his regeneration of the little village.

The good folk of Tomintoul hailed Williams as a saviour and indeed, to them, he was. He created dozens of jobs at his hotel, pub and restaurant, which at one time employed seven chefs, and he sponsored local events including the Tomintoul Highland Games. The villagers had even more reason to believe the Lord had provided. For Williams invested £70,000 on acquiring the title Laird before taking over Tomintoul. Not content with one feudal title, Williams bought himself another eight at a cost of £144,000.

When the Laird of Tomintoul was finally arrested, the villagers could only speak well of him. 'I know what he did was wrong but it wasn't that bad,' said George McAllister, in charge of the local museum. He went on:

> Most of these fraud types spirit the money away into foreign bank accounts or investments abroad but he didn't. He put most of it back here into our wee village. It really made Tomintoul a better place. I found Tony a very charming man, very friendly, with no put-on about him at all. It's hard to understand why a clever person like him would do what he did, but he certainly benefited the village. A lot of the properties have been beautifully restored. Just look around you.

Iain Birnie, running the village shop, said: 'So it was money from London? Big deal. They've got enough of the stuff down there anyway. It should be coming north. Tony Williams did a damn sight more good with it up here than it would ever have done down south.'

At his wood-carving shop in the village square, Donald Corr said: 'Everyone wondered where the money was coming from. We asked ourselves why was he spending it in a wee little place in the Highlands? He wouldn't have gotten it back in 100 years.'

Williams's investment in the village gained him a different kind of dividend, however: disgrace and prison. His downfall came when banks grew suspicious about the large and endless amounts of cash he was depositing. It was believed something more sinister than downright fraud was afoot. So, as obliged to under the Drugs Trafficking Offences Act, they disclosed their worries to the police. Williams's arrest came in July 1994. Two months later he was dismissed from his job.

At his trial, Williams pleaded guilty to seventeen charges of theft from the Receiver of Scotland Yard and two charges of theft from the civilian staff's welfare fund. He initially denied any charges relating to the welfare fund – simply, said his barrister James Sturman, because he had forgotten all about the crime. Williams asked for 535 other charges to be taken into consideration. In all, he had stolen £5,320,737 of the £7,413,761 entrusted to him over the years.

It had been a relief to Williams when he was finally caught, said Mr Sturman. Apart from a few panic-struck lies and half-truths when first arrested, Williams had fully cooperated with the police. Around £529,000 of the stolen funds had been recovered and there were hopes of a further £200,000 to £300,000, the court heard. The lawyer added that Williams felt terrible remorse for his sins and had expressed as much to priests. 'He has lied to his wife, he has lied to his friends, he has lived a lie,' said Mr Sturman.

Referring to his double life in Scotland, prosecuting counsel Brian Barker QC summed up Williams's influence on the Highland village he had changed out of all recognition. 'The suburban civil servant became, when he crossed the border, a nobleman and benefactor of Tomintoul,' he said.

Despite continuing support and some quiet admiration for the accused, Williams did not call any character witnesses. He told the court: 'I don't want to put my good friends in the box to say I was honest. Obviously, I haven't been for years.' Sentencing him to six and a half years for the thefts from his employers and one year for stealing from the welfare fund, the Recorder of London, Sir Lawrence Verney, told him: 'Such crimes are inexcusable. No one minded to follow your example must be left in any doubt as to the consequences.'

Williams, still bearing a healthy tan from his travels, left the dock to begin his sentence, clutching the carrier bag which contained what seemed to be his only worldly goods. His 47-year-old wife vowed to stand by him. She did so and, a mere three years later, the couple were seen strolling hand in hand near the open prison from where he was shortly to be allowed early release, having served only half his sentence – and with only a fraction of the missing £5million recovered.

Two investigations were launched into just how Williams got away with his criminal activities for so long, one concentrating on the civil welfare fund, the other on the secret fund. They did not make happy reading for the red-faced top brass at Scotland Yard. Williams himself had a brief but succinct explanation for his crimes. In a rare interview, he told *The Times* of London: 'I discovered this bloody great bucketful of money. I went from the need to pay off a few debts to what can only be described as greed. There are no excuses.'

Meanwhile, the folk of Tomintoul had been left to pick up the pieces of a property explosion which no longer had limitless funds to sustain it. Jobs were lost and fewer lavish shindigs graced the £25,000 carpet of the bar of the Gordon Hotel. But the village devised one final reminder of the high-living fraudster: a new brand of ale cheekily labelled 'Laird of Tomintoul Beer' and bearing a label in the shape of a Metropolitan Police helmet.

Brazen Burglars who
'Mass Produced' the Mona Lisa

The enigmatic smile on the face of the *Mona Lisa* holds a secret that has intrigued art lovers for centuries. But Leonardo da Vinci's masterpiece once put a broad smile on other faces too – those of three wily fraudsters who stole the painting in one of the most ingenious heists of all time.

The *Mona Lisa* is the most famous portrait in the history of art and, although more than 500 years old, the lady with the ambiguous half-smile continues to fascinate, inspire and cause intense debate. Painted in oil on a panel of poplar wood around 1505, its proper title is *Portrait of Lisa Gherardini, Wife of Francesco del Giocondo*, but in France she is known as *La Joconde,* in Italy *La Gioconda*, and throughout the rest of the world she is simply the *Mona Lisa*.

Housed in the Louvre, Paris, the notion that anyone should be so bold as to plan the theft of what is surely the world's most recognisable painting seemed unthinkable – but not to the three villains who, in 1911, planned to spirit it away from its high-security home in order to create unlimited forged copies. The trio were French art forger and former picture restorer Yves Chaudron, Argentinean trickster and self-styled marquis Eduardo de Valfierno and Italian burglar Vincenzo Peruggia.

Chaudron and Valfierno had been partners in crime for many years. Their nefarious careers began at the turn of the twentieth century in South America where they would offer to steal a painting for a crooked dealer, who would then sell it on to a client without too many questions being asked. This is how their amazing scam worked…

Chaudron and Valfierno would visit a gallery in the guise of supposed art experts (which, in a way, they were). They would target a particular painting and chat about its merits with the gallery owner. On a second visit, they would return armed with a forgery of the 'target' painting, brilliantly executed by Chaudron. This time, he and Valfierno would ask permission to examine the work more closely. When it was taken down from the wall, the deceitful duo would surreptitiously line the back of the canvas with the forgery.

On their third visit to the gallery, they would bring along the crooked dealer. While again examining the painting, the dealer would be invited to make a mark on the back of the canvas – but would, of course, be marking the back of the fake. On their fourth and final visit to the gallery, Chaudron and Valfierno would craftily remove the marked forgery.

The gallery officials were never aware of their part in the confidence trick, since the genuine article remained in place. The crooked dealer, however, always greedily handed over the promised sum for the 'stolen' work of art. If the dealer or the eventual purchaser of the forgery ever wondered why the original painting still hung on the gallery wall, Chaudron and Valfierno would let it be known that a copy of the original had taken its place while the theft was being investigated.

In fact, as well as being great forgers, they were also great judges of human character. They knew it was unlikely that the people they had tricked would ever realise the copies they had purchased were fakes. Even if they suspected it, their pride and vanity would generally persuade them that they were too smart to be duped. And, after all, if it ever dawned on the dealers or the clients that they had been conned, they could hardly go to the police to admit being part of the shady deal.

Since Chaudron specialised in faking the work of Spanish artist Bartolomé Esteban Murillo, it did not take too many months before Argentina – where he and Valfierno were then operating – became flooded with phony Murillos. They moved on to Mexico City, where they perfected their techniques, even providing specially printed 'newspaper cuttings' reporting on the supposed thefts of the works they had replicated and sold. When Mexico City became too hot for the crooks, they headed for Paris. There, they naturally enough visited the world's most renowned art gallery, the Louvre Museum, and espied the world's most famous painting, the *Mona Lisa*.

The scam dreamed up by Yves Chaudron and Eduardo de Valfierno was of epic proportions. They realised they needed a third member for their gang, and recruited Vincenzo Peruggia, a small-time Italian crook who had once worked in the Louvre as a handyman. He knew his way around the gallery and had even put the glass in the screen that protected Leonardo da Vinci's masterpiece. Unbelievably, the gang of three then plotted to steal the *Mona Lisa*.

On Sunday, 20 August 1911, Peruggia, who was dressed as a workman, coolly wandered into the Louvre and secreted himself in the basement. After dark, he emerged from hiding and removed the *Mona Lisa* from the wall, discarded the frame and hid the painting, which measures just 77cm by 53 cm (30in by 21in), under his smock. Within minutes, he vanished into the Parisian night and, by morning, Chaudron and Valfierno were handed the art world's ultimate prize.

28

The painting's disappearance was soon discovered, yet the police were not called because museum officials assumed that it had been taken to the Louvre's in-house studio for a scheduled photographic session for the creation of a new brochure. It wasn't until the Tuesday that the alarm was raised, police were called and the embarrassing gap on the wall of the Louvre became a major news story worldwide.

One of the many theories surrounding its disappearance revolved around the renowned artist Pablo Picasso, who was said to have previously unknowingly purchased stolen artworks from a friend and might have also bought the *Mona Lisa*. Detectives drew a blank but, refusing to abandon this strange line of inquiry, they arrested Picasso's friend, French poet Guillaume Apollinaire, and held him for a week on suspicion of selling the painting before finally releasing him.

Meanwhile, the *Mona Lisa* was far away and, strangely, in perfectly safe hands. At the time they had stolen the painting, the gang already had several prospective clients lined up. For, although it would have been a simple task to sell the genuine *Mona Lisa*, the thieves had a more ambitious plan. They would sell the masterpiece not once but over and over again – and not one of the paintings they unloaded would be the original article. Before the year 1911 was out, no fewer than six American millionaires had each paid $300,000 for what they thought was da Vinci's masterpiece. It mattered little to them that the work had been stolen from the Louvre, greed having overcome any feelings of guilt when seizing upon such a priceless work at such a knockdown price.

Chaudron and Valfierno made almost $2million selling their six expertly forged copies – but they never got the chance to dispose of the real painting. The newly hired member of the trio, Peruggia, grew greedy and ran off to Italy with the genuine article. After two years in hiding, he finally tried to sell it. On 10 December 1913, using the alias Leonardo Vincenzo, he entered the Florence offices of art dealer Alfredo Geri and told him he had the *Mona Lisa* but that, as a self-proclaimed patriot, he believed the masterpiece belonged not in the Louvre but in an Italian museum. He wished to return it to Italy – but wanted 500,000 lire for his troubles.

Although highly sceptical, Geri agreed to view the painting the next day at Peruggia's hotel room, where he arrived with his friend Giovanni Poggi, director of Florence's famous Uffizi Gallery. There, they watched in astonishment as Peruggia removed the painting from the false bottom of an old trunk. The two art experts told Peruggia they must first check the authenticity of the painting before they could buy it. The dim thief gave Geri and Poggi permission to take the painting to a museum and, as he waited patiently in his hotel room, police pounced and arrested him. The trail then led to Chaudron and Valfierno, and the three crooks found themselves in jail.

The *Mona Lisa* was returned to the Louvre where, behind thick glass panels, wired to several alarm systems and under armed guard, the masterpiece remains to this day. However, one lingering doubt remains about the world's most famous painting. No fewer than sixty other alleged *Mona Lisas* have been catalogued in various corners of the world. And they are not all forgeries. Most are believed to be genuine and are attributed, if not to Leonardo da Vinci himself, then to his school of painting. So no one can be absolutely sure that the *Mona Lisa* hanging in the Louvre is the one and only original. Can that be the reason for the lady's mysterious smile?

Joyce McKinney
Kinky Lady who Kidnapped for Love

It began on 14 September 1977 with a brief statement from Scotland Yard. Nothing too dramatic, but enough to arouse the curiosity of a few seasoned crime reporters. A young Mormon missionary, said the Yard, had vanished 'in most unusual circumstances'. The spokesman added: 'We cannot rule out the possibility that he has been abducted.'

Probing deeper, the journalists discovered that the American missionary's name was Kirk Anderson, aged 21, from Salt Lake City. He had apparently received a call from a man called Bob Bosler, who had expressed an interest in turning to Anderson's faith. The young priest had met Bosler at the Mormon church in East Ewell, Surrey, and joined him and a friend to show them the mile-long route to the church offices. None of the three had been seen since.

So far, the story was intriguing, though hardly front-page news. Within hours, however, new revelations had Fleet Street's editors champing at the bit. Salt Lake City Police wired Scotland Yard to warn that before visiting Britain, Anderson had suffered persistent harassment from an admiring female. Even more fascinating was the suggestion from Mormon Church officials that he had been kidnapped because he 'scorned a wealthy woman's love'. It appeared the woman concerned had hired a small army of private detectives to pursue him across America. The trip to Britain was his way of escaping her.

Within three days, Kirk Anderson turned up and confirmed that the story was true. The woman and an accomplice had kept him handcuffed and manacled for seventy-two hours in a remote cottage. Detective Chief Superintendent Hucklesby, head of the CID 'Z' Division, announced that police were searching for two Americans travelling as man and wife. One was Keith Joseph May, alias Bob Bosler, alias Paul Van Deusen, aged 24. The other was Joyce McKinney, alias Cathy Vaughn Bare, alias Heidi Krazler, aged 27. She had long blonde hair and a strong Southern accent. Hucklesby was asked by journalists if it would be right to describe McKinney as attractive? 'Oh yes,' he replied. 'Very.'

31

Later that same day the two suspects were picked up by police in the West Country driving along the A30. Officers had also discovered the secluded holiday cottage near Okehampton, Devon, where Anderson claimed he had been held in chains. There were already rumours coming out of Devon that 'unusual discoveries' at the cottage had left the local police in stitches. Understandably, Hucklesby found himself swamped with questions from the excited media pack. Off the record, he admitted that the Devon and Cornwall Constabulary had found 'certain equipment' at the cottage. 'I can't go into details,' he quipped, 'but I'll tell you what. I've never been lucky enough to have anything like that happen to me.'

A week after the story first broke, McKinney, described as a 'former beauty queen', and Keith May, a trainee architect, appeared in court accused of forcibly abducting and imprisoning Kirk Anderson and possessing an imitation .38 revolver with intent to commit an offence. The 'Sex In Chains' scandal was well underway.

At her next appearance, Joyce McKinney – or Joy as she preferred to be known – showed she could milk publicity to the limit. As the police van drew up outside Epsom Magistrates Court, she managed to fling four notes at the waiting pressmen. They read: 'Please tell the truth. My reputation is at stake!', 'He had sex with me for four days', 'Please get the truth to the public. He made it look like kidnapping' and 'Ask Christians to pray for me.' There then ensued a battle as Joyce, wearing a flimsy cheesecloth outfit with loose neckline, tried to make a dash towards the reporters. Police restrained her but, in the melee, she managed to reveal her ample breasts to photographers. Clearly, McKinney was in no mood to let British justice take its normal course.

Over the next few weeks, the police became increasingly baffled by the bizarre case. Not least was McKinney's claim that, far from locking up the missionary for four days in a Devon love nest, she, May and Anderson had twice been out shopping and dining together in London's West End.

The court committal hearing opened in November 1977 with the prosecution explaining how McKinney had developed a 'consuming desire' for Anderson when they first met in Provo, Utah. They had sex but as this was contrary to Mormon beliefs, Anderson later told her the relationship was over. She refused to accept his decision, blaming the doctrine of his church, and so began her epic attempt to pursue and seduce him. When the trail led to England, McKinney and May, described as her friend and mentor, hatched a plot to kidnap the missionary at gunpoint and drive him to Devon.

In the witness box, Anderson took up the story. He told how he had been chained spreadeagled to the four corners of the bed, after which McKinney ripped off his pyjamas, performed oral sex on him to arouse him and then proceeded to full intercourse. Later they had two further sessions of lovemaking.

Anderson went on: 'She said she was going to get what she wanted, whether I wanted to or not. She said she might keep me there for another month or so until she missed her period.'

McKinney's counsel, Stuart Elgrod, was unimpressed:

> Elgrod: 'I am suggesting that at no stage were you ever tied up in that cottage except for the purpose of sex games.'
>
> Anderson: 'No, no, that's wrong.'
>
> Elgrod: 'The next day you were joking about it. It came off with a can opener. You were completely unfettered.'
>
> Anderson: 'I was bolted in.'
>
> Elgrod: 'You didn't even try to escape?'
>
> Anderson: 'No, I knew I was going back soon anyway.'

The case was adjourned and lawyers from both sides decamped to consider strategy. It certainly didn't look good for the prosecution. Anderson had admitted asking McKinney to rub his back. He also agreed that he had thrown his so-called jailer across the bed in a fit of pique. Then there was the trip to London during his 'confinement' when he, McKinney and May had lunched at the Hard Rock Cafe. It hardly sounded like the experience of a man captured and held against his will.

McKinney was now spilling her side of the story to police. She told how she and Anderson had enjoyed a three-year relationship in which he had made much of the running. How she had stocked up on his favourite food at the Devon cottage. How she bought his blue pyjamas, complete with name tag, and packed herself see-through nighties. And how she even remembered to bring the quilt on which she and Kirk first had sex. She had dreamed up the bondage game, she said, after studying the books of Dr Alex Comfort, author of *The Joy of Sex*, and talking to men with 'sexual hang-ups' in an attempt to understand why Anderson had spurned her. McKinney said:

> They [the men] had said the sexual bondage game, where the woman was the aggressor, was the way to get over the guilt feelings of men who do not enjoy intercourse. When I came to England, I was looking for a real romantic cottage where we could have a honeymoon, and I decided to play some of those bondage games with him. We had such a fun time – just like old times.

Despite her protestations of innocence, Epsom magistrates decided she did have a case to answer. They committed her for a full Crown Court trial but also granted her request to make a statement in court. McKinney jumped at the chance and produced a fourteen-page document which covered her life story. In her strong Southern drawl, she spoke of her conversion to Mormonism while studying at the Tennessee State University, her love affair with Anderson, her bizarre methods of satisfying his sexual guilt complex and, finally, how she became a Mormon outcast. Her statement ended:

> This man has imprisoned my heart with false promises of love and marriage and a family life. He has had me cast into prison for a kidnap he knows he set things up for. I don't want anything more to do with Kirk. He does not know what eternal love is. All I ask is that you do not allow him to imprison me any longer. Let me pick up the pieces of my life.

The court agreed to bail on sureties put up by McKinney's mother, a former English teacher back home in North Carolina, and at last she was free. She became an instant celebrity, being escorted to the finest restaurants by reporters and photographed wherever she went in London. Behind the scenes, a hectic auction was going on as the press clamoured for the rights to sell her life story. The bidding, she advised, ought to start at £50,000.

While in London in 1978, she was photographed at a movie premiere with Keith Moon of The Who, a hedonistic drummer who would soon be dead of a drug overdose. They were cheek to cheek, with one of McKinney's arms around his neck. It was a heady lifestyle for the girl from Avery County, North Carolina, and it could not last. The media wanted to keep the story hot but the forthcoming trial meant they were heavily constrained as to what they could print. Inevitably, they used the time to dig for further background and it was in Los Angeles, where in 1975 McKinney had been chasing Anderson, that they found it.

McKinney had needed to pay the private detectives she had hired to follow his movements. She took to posing for bondage magazines and then graduated to providing sexual services for, as she put it, an 'upper-income clientele'. One of her adverts in the *Los Angeles Free Press* read: 'Fantasy Room. Your fantasy is her speciality! S&M [sadomasochism], B&D [bondage and dominance], escort service, PR work, acting jobs, nude wrestling/modelling, erotic phone calls, dirty panties or pictures, TV charm schools fantasies etc.' The advert closed with a PS: 'Joey says: "Ah love shy boys, dirty ol' men and sugah daddies!"' The enterprise earned her around $50,000 dollars a year.

While McKinney was awaiting trial, a file of photographs showing her performing perverted sexual acts was obtained by the London *Daily Mirror*. The newspaper sat on its exclusive – but, as it turned out, the subject was to provide an even bigger story. As her trial date neared, she and Keith May packed their fourteen suitcases, picked up their British passports (made out in false identities) and flew to Shannon Airport in Ireland. From there, posing as deaf mutes, they flew to Canada and later slipped back across the United States border.

McKinney stayed on the run for fifteen months before the FBI tracked her down in North Carolina. The authorities ended up declining to pursue her extradition but she was convicted of using false passports, given three years' probation and fined. It looked as if the errant manhunter had learned her lesson and might just stay out of trouble. It was not to be. In June 1984, McKinney was arrested in Salt Lake City and accused of disturbing the peace by 'shadowing' Kirk Anderson. Her former lover complained that she had been following and photographing him. McKinney retorted that she was simply writing a book and wanted to know what he was doing with his life. The case was thrown out of court after her lawyer entered a plea of 'extremely not guilty'.

That, it seemed, was the end of her extraordinary story. But inevitably the insuppressible McKinney could be counted on to make further news. In 2008, a 58-year-old woman by the name of Joyce Bernann hit the headlines by offering to pay $50,000 to have puppies cloned from her dead pet dog Booger. Tissue from the ear of her beloved pit bull terrier, frozen after Booger died, was used by a South Korean laboratory to produce five pups. She said she had gone public with her efforts to replicate the dog so that she could be seen 'as someone trying to do something good.'

The media wanted to know more about the mysterious pet lover and discovered that she was none other than the infamous sex abductor, using her middle name Bernann. Moreover, it was revealed that Joyce Bernann McKinney was being sought on charges of plotting a bizarre burglary back in the US. She had missed a 2004 court appearance in Carter County, Tennessee, where she was accused of instructing a 15-year-old boy to break into a house because she needed funds to help another animal … her three-legged horse. According to her lawyer, she had hoped to get money to buy a false leg for the animal.

It also emerged that she was behind a blizzard of writs in her home town of Newland, North Carolina, as she attempted to sue everyone from a magistrate to a police officer to her own parents – in the latter case, over a bee sting to one of her dogs. Writs then flowed in her direction after she fled the town on bail and allegedly refused to pay the fees of three lawyers. When confronted by reporters, Bernann broke down in tears and admitted she was indeed the former beauty queen who had made the headlines in the 1970s as a 'Sex Slave Kidnapper'.

Her cover as Joyce Bernann having been blown, in 2010 McKinney's story was played out over ninety minutes in an American documentary titled *Tabloid*, in which she appeared happily narrating her early days as a North Carolina girl, a Wyoming beauty queen and a Utah university scientist graduate before her obsession with Kirk Anderson made her infamous. True to form, a year later she sued the filmmakers for defamation, saying: 'I had no idea they were going to do this trashy movie.' Her suit was thrown out by the Californian Court of Appeal.

More recent headlines on McKinney were more muted. In 2020, Los Angeles newspapers reported that a 69-year-old woman driver had been charged with accidentally running down and killing a 91-year-old man as he walked his dog in the San Fernando Valley. A judge ruled her incompetent to stand trial and referred her to the Los Angeles County mental health system.

It was a tragic final chapter in the almost unbelievable story of the woman who, in the film *Tabloid*, mused: 'I could never understand the public's fascination with my love life. I'm not a movie star. I'm just a human being that was caught in an extraordinary circumstance.'

Charles Ingram and Charles Van Doren
TV Quiz Cheats

It's the last place on Earth that you'd expect a conman to operate: under the glare of television studio lights and with an audience of millions watching every move. Yet the quiz show *Who Wants To Be A Millionaire?* was constantly targeted by clever scam merchants trying to cheat their way to the magic millions on offer.

From the moment it first aired in Britain in 1998, the show was a huge hit, attracting audiences of up to nineteen million, a third of the then population, and its format was exported all over the globe. But with so much money up for grabs it quickly attracted con-artists – although it was not until two decades later, during research for a TV drama about the phenomenon, that it was revealed how chiselers had netted at least ten per cent of the £50million prize money paid out in those early years. Most of the misappropriated winnings went to cheats who managed to manipulate the phone-line application process to get on the show. Having achieved that, they would get expert tuition in answering the likeliest questions with textbook answers. And when they needed to call for help in the crucial 'Phone a Friend' round, the 'friend' was actually a quick-thinking researcher with reference books to hand.

The most blatant trickster, however, cheated his way to the £1million prize in an extraordinarily novel way. He was British Army officer Charles Ingram who, like all contestants, had to answer fifteen multiple choice questions to reach the magic million in 2001. One incorrect reply would cost him dear but Major Ingram, although bumbling his way through the multiple choices, eventually picked every single correct answer.

Tension in the studio reached fever pitch when quizmaster Chris Tarrant posed the £500,000 question: 'Baron Haussmann is best known for the planning of which city?' Ingram correctly answered: 'Paris'. This brought him to the £1million question: 'A number 1 followed by 100 zeros is known by what name?' The four alternative answers offered were: (a) Googol, (b) Megatron, (c) Gigabit and (d) Nanomol.

37

Ingram took his time as the audience held its breath – apart from a couple who, throughout the show, had been intermittently coughing. Ingram puzzled aloud, evaluating each option before finally answering: 'Googol'. Tarrant gave the contestant a big hug and, to riotous applause, handed him his seven-figure cheque.

Unbeknown to the audience, however, panic reigned. Tarrant was called away by the producer and told that suspicions had been raised that coughs from the audience were a secretly coded series of prompts to help Ingram reach his goal. The major was asked to hand back his cheque.

The man whose fleeting fame and fortune were replaced by ignominy and ruin had indeed been in cahoots with those coughing members of the audience, one of whom was his wife Diana. Married for a dozen years and with three daughters, the couple had found themselves £50,000 in debt and without a home of their own, since they had always been housed in Army quarters. The ambitious Diana decided that if they couldn't earn their way to a grander lifestyle, they would simply have to win one. Aided by her brother Adrian, she bombarded the *Who Wants To Be A Millionaire?* premium-rate phone lines to gain a place on the show and even practised on a mock keyboard to maximise their chances of getting through the preliminary 'fastest finger first' round. Their perseverance paid off and in 2001 Adrian and then Diana appeared as contestants and won £32,000 each.

Charles Ingram then won himself a place on the show and, in September 2001, got the chance to sit in the same seat that his wife had occupied earlier in the year. He appeared to be the perfect contestant, laughing and joking with quizmaster Tarrant as he correctly answered the early, simpler questions, from £100 upwards. By the time he got to the £8,000 question, however, studio floor managers working for the programme-makers Celador were already warning that 'something strange was going on'. A camera was kept trained on Diana Ingram, seated high in the audience. Unaware that her every move was being recorded, she was seen to cough twice to signal the correct answer to the £32,000 question.

The next bout of coughing came from a different quarter: a fellow contestant awaiting his turn in the front row just 10ft away. Tecwen Whittock, a bespectacled college lecturer, seemed to be prompting Ingram when Tarrant came to read the correct options to the top money-making questions. It allowed Ingram correctly to attribute the painting *The Ambassadors* to Holbein, winning himself £125,000. The next question was: 'What type of garment is an Anthony Eden?' As Ingram pondered, Whittock coughed three times and Ingram became £250,000 richer by correctly answering: 'A hat'.

By this time, the production team was watching both Tecwen Whittock and Diana Ingram like hawks. The camera trained on Mrs Ingram revealed some extraordinary reactions. She appeared to be fuming that her husband was overplaying his hand and that he had gone on beyond the £125,000 question. And, as he launched himself into the £1million question, she was heard to mutter: 'Oh God, don't start'.

So intent was Chris Tarrant on doing his job that he was wholly unaware of the drama being played out around him. When Ingram correctly responded to the final question with the answer 'Googol', the TV host beamed: 'You are the most amazing contestant we have ever, ever had. I have no idea how you got there.' Urging the audience into rapturous applause, he added: 'I have no idea what your strategy was; you were so brave. I am so proud to have met you. You are just an amazing human being.'

Fortunes have been won and lost with alacrity in the murky world of crime but none so fleetingly as that bestowed upon Charles Ingram. His loss of fortune led to sudden shame and a summons to court where, in March 2003, 39-year-old Ingram, his 38-year-old wife and Tecwen Whittock, aged 53, were accused of 'procuring a valuable security by deception' by dishonestly getting Tarrant to sign the £1million cheque. A recording of the show replayed in court showed Ingram musing aloud about the possible answers to each question – and Whittock coughing as he mentioned the correct one. It was suggested that Diana coughed when co-conspirator Whittock appeared not to know the answer himself. Predictably, when Whittock got his own turn in the hot seat immediately after Ingram, his cough disappeared. So, it seems, did his skill at answering the questions, for after risking all for the major, he himself walked away with only £1,000.

The prosecution suggested that the coughing ploy was a back-up to another, more sophisticated plot that had gone wrong. The Ingrams, it was alleged, had practised a high-tech scheme in which the correct answers would be sent to the major via four vibrating pagers hidden about his person. The prosecution suggested that the Ingrams' intended scam involved planting a stooge in the audience who would have a mobile phone with the line permanently open to another accomplice outside the studio. This fourth person could hear the questions, look up the answers and send the right responses to the pagers: one bleeper for each of the four multiple-choice answers. Just hours before he went into the hot seat, messages were being sent from the major's mobile to the four pagers, but by the time Ingram appeared on the show, the plan had been abandoned as being too risky.

After twenty-two days in court and still protesting their innocence, the conspirators were found guilty but were spared prison, being given suspended jail sentences and fines of between £10,000 and £30,000. Describing the plot as a 'shabby schoolboy trick', the judge told Ingram: 'You certainly had no notion that it would result in you going on to win £1million but somehow, more by good luck than good management, it did.' Turning to Diana, he added: 'You might be well advised to thank your lucky stars you are not going to prison today and put aside any childish wishes of bravado that you are entitled to this money.'

The judge's entreaty went unheeded, the Ingrams making a further string of television appearances, this time legitimately, to proclaim the unfairness of the verdict. There was a brief fillip in their fortunes when the canned episode of *Who Wants To Be A Millionaire?* was finally shown and seventeen million viewers tuned in to watch it in Britain alone. The couple gained a fleeting celebrity status across the Atlantic, where they were invited onto TV talk shows. A proposed movie about the case never transpired and it was not until 2020 that the TV drama *Quiz* was made about their misadventures, revealing that they were only two among many shady contestants – and, ignominiously, were possibly the least successful. However, the series did at last give a somewhat sympathetic view of the major who was a millionaire for only minutes – and, he said, gave him and his wife some hope that one day their names would be cleared of such a devious deception.

Charles Ingram was not the first high-profile quiz show contestant to become infamous for cheating – and almost beating – the system. For a brief period in the late 1950s, a respectable, clean-cut, all-American academic named Charles Van Doren became one of the most popular celebrities in the United States.

Van Doren, a 30-year-old lecturer at Columbia University, was an ambitious egghead whose brilliant mind gained him an invitation to appear on the popular television show of the time, *Twenty One*. Contestants were placed in a sound-proofed box then bombarded with questions, the answers to which became increasingly and nail-bitingly difficult.

Unlike most contestants, Van Doren, who first appeared in January 1957, came up trumps week after week, accumulating an ever-growing mountain of cash and a fan following of millions hooked on the show. He did not make his role look easy, however. After quizmaster Jack Barry had asked him a particularly difficult question, his brow would furrow. Beads of sweat would build on his temple as he stared intently at the floor – moments of seemingly mental torture that made the show an astounding success.

Every week the same team of Jack Barry and Charles Van Doren would have the audience at home and in the studio perched on the edge of their seats as the tension built to its inexorable climax. As the last crucial question was answered, the quizmaster would shout 'Correct' and the audience would howl with delight. At the end of an incredible fifteen-week run, Van Doren had won more than $129,000 worth of prizes, a small fortune in those days. This was not such a feat, however, because before going on air, the producers had supplied him with every answer. Even his nail-biting responses had been carefully rehearsed.

Van Doren had not always been such a cheat. When first invited onto the show, he had spurned the suggestion that he be given clues to the answers. He relented when a persuasive producer pandered to his vanity, telling him that by 'helping glamourise intellectualism' he could set a fine example to the youth of America. And like an addict, once he had begun to cheat, he found there was no turning back. After all, it seemed to be a scam in which no one was getting hurt.

Van Doren almost got away with the fraud. It wasn't a television watchdog who caught him out, however; it was one of his fellow contestants. This whistleblower, Joseph Stempel, had been a quiz regular before Van Doren and had been equally successful – because he too had been supplied with the answers. When Van Doren joined him on the show, he overshadowed Stempel, and the 30-year-old New Yorker was asked to bow out. Astonishingly, Stempel at first agreed and dutifully gave an incorrect answer to end his run of success. But as he watched his former rival stashing away a small fortune week after week, he changed his mind and reported the quiz show's shameful secret. He said: 'I got tired of being in the shadows. Once I saw Van Doren, I knew my days on the show were numbered. He was tall, thin and "waspy". I was this Bronx Jewish kid. It was as simple as that.'

Van Doren's *Twenty One* run ended when he lost to Vivienne Nearing, a lawyer whose husband he had previously beaten. But because of his celebrity status, he was offered a three-year contract with NBC News as a special 'cultural correspondent' for the flagship *Today* programme. His career in television was short-lived. When the *Twenty One* fraud was exposed by Stempel and others, Van Doren at first attempted to lie his way out of trouble. He denied any wrongdoing, saying: 'It's silly and distressing to think that people don't have more faith in quiz shows.'

His weasel words failed to convince. The press, the public and, of course, rival television stations were outraged. Even President Dwight D. Eisenhower publicly condemned the cynical deception. He ordered an investigation by the Justice Department and Van Doren was interrogated by a grand jury. But when faced with the might of a congressional sub-committee in November 1959, he broke down and confessed all, saying that the show had 'ballooned beyond my wildest dreams' and that 'this went to my head'.

Charles Van Doren escaped a prison sentence but lost his post with Columbia University and became a reclusive author of academic works. He died in 2019 but despite his disgrace did not seem to have suffered financially through his years in the wilderness. For after his brief but celebrated career as a television star, no one had ever asked the flawed quiz king to hand back his prize money.

Peter Foster
Wild Life of the Wily Wizard of Oz

When arch conman Peter Foster announced that he was writing his autobiography, there were groans from those around the world whom he'd duped over the years. The rich, the powerful, the sadly impoverished and, more generally, the plain gullible did not wish to be reminded of how they had been taken for a ride. Their nervousness about Foster's announcement in the summer of 2020 that he was about to 'tell all' was heightened by the fear that the cheery charlatan's ability to embellish the facts might make them look even more stupid than they had actually been.

If Peter Clarence Foster did not exist, it would be hard for anyone to invent him. Even as a character in fiction, the role would be just too implausible. Yet this affable but, at first sight, unimpressive Australian somehow has the gift to persuade even the most sceptical and cynical individuals to part with their natural caution – and, of course, their money.

Foster's craft is seemingly effortless, which is the mark of a great confidence trickster. While appearing not to have a care in the world, he will be coolly plotting to ensnare his next victim. No detail is too small and no target too big for him. He has hoodwinked get-rich-quick merchants, charity workers, prisoners in jail, warders in charge of them, shopkeepers, hotels, credit card companies, beautiful models, hard-headed businessmen, lawyers and politicians. At the pinnacle of his career, he even sucked the British Prime Minister and his family into his web of deceit. And all done so effortlessly, with a cheeky smile, a merry quip and a glass of champagne in hand.

Foster is, in the words of one of his old school friends, 'a likeable bastard'. His home territory is Australia's Gold Coast, that strip of high-rise beach-side high life that glitters on the Pacific shores of Queensland and is the holiday haunt of bikini-clad beauties and bleached-haired surfers. Foster could have been one of the latter but his ambition drove him at an early age away from the golden beaches and into the hotel bars of the town of Surfers Paradise. He could have become a respectable businessman, rich through honest dealings, but that was not his way. 'It's not that he couldn't make a living out of running a legitimate business; it was just more fun for him to try to beat the system,' said a former classmate at Aquinas Catholic College. He recalled 15-year-old Foster returning from a family holiday in the Philippines laden down with fake designer watches to sell to fellow pupils.

Once he left school, however, the launch of his entrepreneurial career was inauspicious. His first venture was promoting pop concerts and boxing bouts but he fell foul of the law in 1983 when he was fined £75,000 for trying to defraud an insurance company out of £40,000. The following year, he was declared bankrupt after trying to market a 'magic' method of quitting smoking.

With his reputation sullied in Australia, in 1986, at the age of 24, he flew to Britain seeking to ride to riches on someone else's coat tails. His unwitting target was the country's most desired pin-up, Samantha Fox, famous at the time for her nubile body which graced the pages of calendars, posters and tabloid newspapers. He wooed and won her, not just to make himself the most envied man in Britain but also because he needed a celebrity sponsor to launch his latest 'miracle' slimming potion, Bai Lin Tea. He persuaded Sam to promote the dodgy brew, and over the next ten years the lovebirds travelled the world in style, from Australia to Tokyo to Africa's Safari country. He bought her jewellery, a sports car, a magnificent home and claimed to be deeply in love with her. The cheat was seeing other women on the side, however, and when Sam found out, she dumped him, later referring to him only as 'the rat'.

Meanwhile, Foster had made untold millions out of selling Bai Lin Tea franchises in Britain, taking £5,000 from each of about 100 would-be distributors. However, when the product was labelled a sham by TV hostess Esther Rantzen on her top-rated show *That's Life*, the pyramid selling scam collapsed with debts of £700,000 and Foster's company, Slimweight, ended up in voluntary liquidation.

Foster soon bounced back with a new diet scam, hiring Britain's 1998 Young Slimmer of the Year, Michelle Deakin, to back his next product. Nineteen-year-old Michelle was persuaded to launch the 'Deakin Diet', claiming that she had won her title by taking Foster's cheap pills filled with guar gum. The naive Liverpool girl fell for his soft sell after he wooed her with champagne parties, rides in his Rolls Royce and flights in a private jet. But her claim to have lost weight through the conman's pills was shown to be a transparent lie. As Foster faced trial on trades description charges and the Bai Lin venture collapsed, he fled to Australia in 1987 to be reunited with his doting mother Louise Polleti, long divorced from the conman's father, hotel owner Clarence 'Clarrie' Foster, who died in 1998.

Two years later, he turned up in California, establishing a base in Beverly Hills to peddle another useless slimming product, Chow Lo Tea. Having run up huge advertising debts and serving four months in jail for false claims, he again went on the run. After persuading the Australian consulate in Los Angeles to issue him with a passport, he flew to the Caribbean, then to Australia, much to the annoyance of Los Angeles city attorney Jim Hahn who described him as 'a con-artist peddling snake oil'. Back again in Queensland, Foster devised Biometrics Contour Treatment, which he claimed shrank girls' thighs. He sold a string of franchises before (and after) the Trade Practices Commission banned his business, accusing him of misleading and deceptive conduct.

Foster was now literally running out of places to run to. In 1994 he returned to Britain, supposedly 'to wipe the slate clean' over his previous UK diet scams, including Bai Lin Tea, and pay two outstanding penalties of about £25,000 each, one against himself and one against his mother as chairman of one his companies. He paid only his own – which, as we shall see, was to cause his mother some problems.

On this return visit to Britain, he very publicly kissed and made up with Sam Fox, saying that 'letting her go was the biggest mistake I ever made.' According to Foster, he resumed his affair with her and even planned marriage – claims which shocked Fox fans because since their last romance she had given up nude modelling, started a singing career and a lesbian relationship and had become a born-again Christian. Whether or not his nuptial plans for Ms Fox were genuine, the playboy's hidden agenda was to involve her in his next diet scam. Sam was having none of it and the rekindled romance quickly fizzled out.

Other products were dreamed up. There was Thigh Tone 1, then Body Right Pro which Pamela Anderson, star of American TV series *Baywatch*, was conned into backing. A video was made with a shaky hand-held camera in which Pamela appeared to support the product, and this was about to be used to persuade British punters to buy distributorships when police again pounced. Foster was remanded in custody on the earlier Deakin Diet offences under the Trades Description Act.

At Liverpool Crown Court in January 1996 he was told by the judge: 'I have formed a very unfavourable view of you as someone whose champagne lifestyle meant that as long as you cut a dash or make a splash, you were happy to do so. It may fairly be said that the party is now over.' In fact, the party was only just beginning, although it did not look like it at the time to Peter Foster. Sentenced to two years' jail after which he was to be deported, he was incarcerated in ultra-tough Walton Prison, Liverpool, and later the fortress-like Winson Green, Birmingham.

His mother Louise immediately flew from Australia to comfort her son but never got past Heathrow Airport. When her plane touched down, she was arrested for non-payment of her £25,000 fine. Because her son had gambled away the money set aside to clear her debt, she spent four weeks, including

Christmas, in Holloway Prison. She was eventually freed only when her other child, Jill, organised a whip-round back in Queensland.

Forgiven by his doting mother, Peter launched an appeal which reduced his sentence so that, with remission, he needed to serve only nine months. Happily for him, he was moved to Sudbury open prison, Derbyshire, where his tales of sun, fun and sex in the fast lane made his fellow inmates green with envy – then red with rage when he took some of them for a ride with his phoney promises.

Foster was regularly allowed out with a prison officer to raise funds for the jail's own anti-drugs charity, Outreach, but in August 1996 he walked through the gates and never returned. Why he should go on the run only ten days before he was due to be freed was at first a mystery, although it later emerged that he feared fresh fraud charges were being prepared against him over his Thigh Tone activities. His disappearance from Sudbury was a severe embarrassment for prison officers who had trusted him to work outside the jail on their charity venture. It was also damaging to former inmates whom he had persuaded to work for him on his next planned diet scam and who now feared their parole would be cancelled. And it was financially disastrous to businessmen whom he had already persuaded to hand over money for the project, including, astonishingly, a fellow prisoner at Sudbury who had given him £13,000.

Fugitive Foster first fled to Ireland and then to Australia, where he was again jailed for five months for entering the country on a false passport and inducing witnesses to give false evidence. The judge in the case at Southport District Court, on the Gold Coast, appeared to sympathise with the conman, as ever in contrite and charming mood. Judge John Newton praised his initiative and said: 'As an entrepreneur you have attempted to develop a number of business projects which seem to offer a great deal of scope for success.' The judge even offered his 'best wishes' for the jailbird's next supposed endeavour, Outreach Australia, a project to teach children the dangers of drugs and keep them from a life of crime – an idea he had conveniently borrowed from the warders he had conned at Sudbury Prison. For his part, Foster promised, tongue presumably firmly in cheek, that he would 'endeavour to use my period of incarceration constructively and for the benefit of the community as a whole.' Predictably, as soon as he was released he went back to his old tricks.

So why does Peter Foster bother to take the harsh and rocky route to riches? Why not settle for an honest life as a legitimate businessman, as the Australian judge had suggested when he described the fraudster as an 'entrepreneur'? The answer is supplied by Foster himself, who once told a buddy: 'The money's great but the buzz comes from knowing you've pulled off the sting. It's better than sex.'

Two of those elements came together in his next, most extraordinary sting operation. Arriving back in Britain in 2002, he managed to get close to the highest seat of power in the land: to trick his way into the confidence of Number 10 Downing Street and to be on first-name terms with the prime minister's family – while bedding one of his wife's best friends. It was the pinnacle of his career as a conman. Foster made front-page news after he embroiled Premier Tony Blair and his wife Cherie, a leading barrister, in serious allegations of political sleaze. It emerged that Foster had become the lover of Cherie's closest confidante, her indispensable fashion and lifestyle guru Carole Caplin, and had taken on the role of Mrs Blair's part-time financial adviser. He had used his negotiating skills to purchase two apartments for the Blairs at a bargain price in an upmarket development in Bristol.

It seemed an unbelievable lapse of common sense for Tony Blair to have allowed a conman such control over his family's private affairs. But strenuous denials from Downing Street were soon seen to be a smokescreen as documents proved the closeness of Foster's relationship with the Blairs at the same time as he was using it to entice investors to sink money into his latest dubious slimming venture.

The scam was devilishly clever. Foster had known of Caplin's connection to the prime minister before even meeting her. She was a regular visitor to Downing Street and had even holidayed with the Blairs abroad. She conducted Cherie in fitness workouts, alternative therapy sessions and even chose her clothes. Within three days of Foster engineering an introduction to Caplin at a trendy Chelsea coffee bar in July 2002, the 39-year-old conman and the 42-year-old former topless model were lovers. 'She's quite a babe,' Foster told a pal, 'but more importantly, she knows the Blairs.'

Soon he was boasting to investors in his new company, Renuelle, that he was on target to secure the premier's support for a healthy lifestyle programme aimed at schools. The Children's Education Programme was to be a national tour organised by Renuelle to warn youngsters about the dangers of obesity. With government backing, Foster knew it would win Renuelle instant credibility, enabling him to market his latest quack diet pills, Trimit, through a network of franchisees, some of whom had already paid his company between £25,000 and £75,000.

Meanwhile, Foster had so ingratiated himself with Cherie Blair that she had allowed him to handle the purchase of two £297,000 apartments for her, one for the use of her 18-year-old student son Euan and the other as an investment. The wheeler dealer invoked the Blairs' name to haggle down the price of the properties by £69,000 and arranged to pick up the legal bill for the purchases. The fact that these negotiations on behalf of the Blairs were being enacted only three months after Foster first met Carole Caplin is an indication of just how swiftly he was able to insinuate himself into the lives of his victims.

When news of the property deal leaked out, Downing Street spin doctors went into overdrive to play down the connection between the convicted conman and the prime minister's wife. But protestations from Number 10 were silenced by a string of emails that had already passed between Foster and Mrs Blair at the time of the negotiations in October.

Conveniently released to a newspaper 'from a source in Australia', they made dynamite reading. 'We weren't looking to buy the property but steal it,' Foster told Cherie. Another email read: 'I have spoken to [a property manager] and he will jump through hoops for you. I have reduced his fee. I will keep the pressure on him to perform in double-quick time.' And cosily: 'Let me know if I can be of service. Your pleasure is my purpose – Peter.' Signing herself Cherie, she replied: 'I cannot thank you enough, Peter, for taking over these negotiations for me. I really appreciate it.' Other emails assured him that 'we certainly are on the same wavelength' and 'you're a star'.

The scandal was seen as so dangerous by the British government that, in an unprecedented move, Cherie Blair was forced to take the stage for a televised address to the nation in which, her voice breaking with emotion, she attempted to win the country's sympathy by portraying herself as a normal working mother trying to cope with a busy life. 'I'm not superwoman,' she declared. 'The reality of my daily life is that I'm juggling a lot of balls in the air: trying to be a good wife and mother, trying to be the prime minister's consort at home and abroad, a barrister and a charity worker – and sometimes some of the balls get dropped.' At one point she wept as she explained that she was somehow trying to protect her son by negotiating for the apartments, but the verdict of most newspapers the following day was that hers was a sob story rather than the proper explanation expected of a tough £300,000-a-year leading barrister.

In the midst of this furore, Carole Caplin revealed that she had been made pregnant by Foster but had suffered a miscarriage. She bravely (or foolishly) invited TV cameras into her home to film what turned out to be her boyfriend's last days in Britain. In the documentary, *The Conman, His Lover and the Prime Minister's Wife*, Foster spoke about the storm over the Blairs' apartments, saying: 'I think Cherie has handled a bad situation atrociously and she let it get out of hand.' Asked if she had lied, he added: 'Yeah, yeah, she has.' An even more uncomfortable piece of viewing for Downing Street was when Tony Blair left a midnight message on Miss Caplin's answer machine, beginning: 'Hi, it's Tony calling...'

Throughout this period, Foster was fighting a legal battle against deportation to Australia, which he claimed Cherie Blair was helping him overturn. Indeed, his case papers were faxed to Downing Street for Cherie's perusal. With time running out, and with impatient Trimit pill investors snapping at his heels for repayment of their stake money, Foster left Britain for Dublin before being finally deported from there to Australia. His parting shot to the Blairs was 'Some say power corrupts and maybe power changes people.'

Foster himself seemed a changed man. Having quit Britain in a fit of self-pity, he brightened up when he hit the Gold Coast where, his vows of undying love for Carole Caplin instantly forgotten, he threw himself into a round of carousing with his old mates and new girlfriends. In a Surfers Paradise bar in March 2003, he was filmed taking a call from Carole on his mobile phone – speaking earnestly to her for a few minutes before ending the conversation with the words: 'Trust me, Carole' – then turning back to the semi-clad blonde on his lap!

Meanwhile, the playboy was still hatching plans to separate the gullible from their money. As an ex-associate told the author:

> He will do anything to advance himself and will sacrifice anyone else along the way. He is convinced that eventually his destiny is to be a leader on the world stage. He told me his long-term aim was to find a small country, probably among the Pacific islands, and offer his expertise to its leader to boost that nation's economy. He would do this for nothing in return for being granted ambassadorial status, so that he could hobnob with world politicians and travel the globe with diplomatic immunity.

The boastful conversation was prophetic. In 2006 Foster was being hunted by police in Fiji, where he had established himself as a property developer and had been acting as a 'consultant' to one of the Pacific nation's political parties. On the run over fraud-related charges, Foster, clad only in his underpants, jumped off a bridge on the outskirts of the capital, Suva, but was picked up by a police launch.

A month later, a trusting judge freed him on bail, despite warnings that he was a 'huge flight risk' – which soon proved to be the case. In January 2007, Foster persuaded an Australian yacht crew to ferry him out of Suva, and he was next seen wading ashore on an isolated beach in the neighbouring island nation of Vanatu. He was stripped to the waist and carrying only a pair of sandals and a plastic bag with his possessions.

Outlawed in Fiji, he flew to Queensland, where he faced charges of money laundering and forging bank documents relating to a $Aust300,000 business loan that he had used to cover his own credit card debts and pay his girlfriend's rent. A four-year jail term failed to reform him. Despite a ban on him working in the slimming industry, he got involved in selling a diet spray called SensaSlim. Unfortunately for him, investigators discovered that the Swiss Institut de Reserche Intercontinental that had verified the effectiveness of the spray did not exist! He went on the run again and, when caught, was given a year for contempt of court.

Still not shamed, Foster assumed a new identity as 'Mark Hughes' to lure an investor into spending $Aust1.3million on an offshore betting business named the Sports Trading Company. Accused of fraud and possessing a false passport, he spent eighteen months on remand before again walking free in October 2018. The court's leniency appeared to have made an impression on the serial conman, who settled for a quieter life caring for his mother until she died aged 88 in May 2020. Yet, incredibly, the devoted son was secretly plotting a re-run of his betting scam.

Under the name 'Bill Dawson', Foster formed Sport Predictions to lure investors with the promise of 'fool-proof money-spinning' riches. With police on his tail, he fled 1,000 miles north to a remote Queensland hideaway in Port Douglas where he planned to buy a yacht, presumably in yet another bid to sail to freedom. However, as he walked his dogs on a beach in August 2020, the 57-year-old was rugby tackled to the ground by undercover police posing as joggers. Protesting, his last words before being hauled off to the cells were 'This wasn't necessary!'

For Foster, the good news was that it looked as if he would be getting plenty of time to write his promised autobiography. The bad news was that his customary pleas for leniency were likely to leave courts unimpressed. After all, the arch conman's criminal history had covered a career-long catalogue of criminality and terms of imprisonment in Europe, North America, Australasia and Micronesia.

Early in his disreputable career, Foster had boasted: 'Being a conman is one of the most prestigious professions you can pursue. Every day crackled with excitement as I made millions, models and mayhem.' More recently, he seemed to have changed his mind. When asked by Melbourne's *The Age* newspaper whether he still called himself a conman, he replied: 'International man of mischief is clever and perhaps more accurate.' Yet someone has to be holder of the inglorious title 'The World's Most Notorious Living Conman' and that dishonour deservedly belongs to Peter Clarence Foster.

Wild West's Most Lawless 'Goodies' and 'Baddies'

The Wild West has been portrayed in movies as a glamorous but violent vista of panoramic prairies, cattle, cowboys and gunslingers. Riding this range (when not visiting saloons filled with sassy bargirls) are the characteristic rugged pioneering heroes of America's untamed territories. Classic Westerns depict them as a slick, handsome, gun-toting 'goodies' meting out justice to the foul, scowling, black-hearted 'baddies'.

But was that really how the West was won? Of course not. No one remotely like Roy Rogers or the Lone Ranger actually existed. And the real-life characters whose identities Hollywood borrowed, from Wyatt Earp to Butch Cassidy, were far from being the heroes and anti-heroes portrayed on screen. In fact, the supposed 'goodies' were often worse than the 'baddies'; the cowboys were anything but clean-cut or even clean, their gals even less so, and the forces of law and order were, well, lawless.

Take, for instance, *Butch Cassidy and the Sundance Kid*, played by Paul Newman and Robert Redford in the 1969 movie but in reality never as famous as the fictionalised film suggests. Butch was born Robert LeRoy Parker in Beaver, Utah, in 1866. His mentor, who taught him the art of rustling and horse thieving, was local small-time villain Mike Cassidy, and it was his name that Parker adopted when he nicknamed himself Butch Cassidy.

As a youth, Butch was rarely out of trouble, graduating from petty larceny to bank holdups and train robbery. Inevitably he spent time in prison but when he eventually got parole from Rawlings Penitentiary, Wyoming, he rallied five accomplices and formed his own gang. One of them was Harry Alonzo Longabaugh, a petty thief born in Mont Clare, Pennsylvania, in 1867. Longabaugh labelled himself the Sundance Kid after a spate of horse rustling earned him a spell in Sundance Jail, Cook County, Wyoming.

These renegades perpetrated so many crimes that they became known as the Wild Bunch. Trains were their speciality. They once stole $30,000 from a Union Pacific express by unclipping the rear carriage and blowing open the onboard safe. Three more train robberies followed until finally the famous Pinkerton detectives were hired to hunt them down.

Although nothing like the characters portrayed on the silver screen, both Butch and Sundance had a certain style about them, revelling in their notoriety as they stayed one step ahead of the law. Butch, who was regarded as a cheery, cheeky chappie, was said to have never fired a shot directly at another man. Whenever he was being pursued, he would aim at the horses instead – gentlemanly perhaps but animal rights activists would have strung him up from a tree. Likewise, Sundance had no raindrops falling on his head, only 'Wanted' posters. In 1901 he married his girlfriend Etta Place and, to avoid the bounty hunters on his trail, they fled with Butch to South America where, in Argentina, Chile and eventually Bolivia, they found rich pickings robbing banks, mines and trains.

In 1908 Butch and Sundance met their fate in San Vincente, southern Bolivia, where, as the film suggests, they were riddled with bullets in a gunfight with local militia. Their final act, however, may have been a joint suicide pact. A police report revealed that both had bullet wounds to the forehead, suggesting that Butch had shot the fatally wounded Sundance to put him out of his misery, then turned the gun on himself.

Another outlaw of the Wild West who was elevated in legend was Charles Earl Boles, known as Black Bart. An aspiring gentleman at heart, he was always well-mannered and respectful, even when breaking the law. Bart would never harm the people he robbed and refused to steal money or jewellery from individuals, choosing instead the safes and mailbags on stagecoaches.

Bart's first recorded holdup was in the summer of 1875. Dressed in a conspicuous white coat, with a flour sack disguising his identity, he ambushed a coach as it struggled up a steep hill near Sonora, California. Poking out from the bushes nearby were, the driver thought, the guns of Bart's accomplices and, apparently outnumbered seven to one, he followed Bart's orders to throw down the treasure box and mailbags. What followed has passed into folklore. A woman passenger was so scared that she threw down her purse at Bart's feet – only for him to calmly pick it up and, with a gracious bow, hand it back to her. It was only later discovered that the 'guns' were merely sticks and that the accomplices whom Bart had loudly ordered to shoot if resistance was offered, were, of course, non-existent.

Bart continued to earn his reputation as the 'Gentleman Bandit' for several years, notching up twenty-eight robberies, his particular trademark being the poetic messages that he sometimes left at the scene of his crimes. He was apprehended only after fleeing wounded from a botched holdup in 1883, leaving a handkerchief with a San Francisco laundry mark by which he was traced. Revealed as a British-born immigrant who had joined the Californian

Gold Rush, Boles, then aged 54, was jailed in San Quentin for a modest four years after returning much of his ill-gotten gains. A police report described him as 'a person of great endurance [who] exhibited genuine wit under most trying circumstances and was extremely proper and polite in behavior. Eschews profanity.'

One of the most infamous gunslingers of the Wild West was the young tearaway known as Billy the Kid. Born Henry McCarty in New York in 1859, he moved with his mother to New Mexico, where he turned to petty crime. Arrested, he escaped jail by climbing up a chimney and went on the trail as a roving ranch hand. A sure-shot with a Winchester rifle and a Colt revolver, in 1877 he killed his first victim during a bust-up in an Arizona saloon. Revelling in his new-found reputation as a gunslinger, he adopted the alias William Bonney and became known as Billy the Kid or simply The Kid.

Over the next four years, the baby-faced outlaw was involved in the deaths of some nine men, at least four of whom he killed single-handedly. His most dramatic venture was an act of revenge for the murder of his employer, a rancher who had befriended him. In 1878 English-born rancher John Tunstall was gunned down in cold blood by two killers hired by a corrupt sheriff named William Brady. The Kid trailed the murderers and shot them dead. With a price on his head, he then teamed up with a gang of gunslingers who assassinated the sheriff and, in what became known as the 'Lincoln County War', spent months in running shoot-outs with the dubious forces of law and order.

The Kid left the 'war' as a local hero with a reputation as the West's 'most wanted' gunman. His notoriety infuriated the governor of New Mexico territory, Lew Wallace, who set out to trick Billy into giving himself up in exchange for a light sentence. The man given the poison chalice of trapping him was The Kid's former friend Pat Garrett, by now made sheriff of Lincoln County as a reward for his treachery. When The Kid turned up he was arrested and sentenced to hang but again escaped from jail, shooting dead two guards.

Pat Garrett finally got his man by lying in wait at the home of a mutual friend. When Billy the Kid walked in, Garrett fired two shots from his revolver, piercing the fugitive's heart. The Kid became an instant folk hero, his reputation enhanced by the boast that he had killed twenty-one men, one for each year of his life. Although the tally was more likely 'only' nine, Hollywood took his fame to new levels with dozens of movies, along with hundreds of songs, books and television programmes – depictions of the outlaw in popular culture fluctuating between cold-blooded killer and young champion fighting for justice.

If any one person epitomises the disparity between the depiction of the Wild West's most famous sons as dastardly villains or folk heroes, it is Jesse Woodson James. Was he, as moviemakers and folklore have it, a Robin Hood of the West or merely a murderous psychopath who killed to line his own pockets?

Jesse James, born in 1847, and his brother Frank four years older, were raised by their poverty-stricken mother in a log cabin in Kearney, Missouri. The state suffered split loyalties when the American Civil War broke out in 1861 and the James boys chose the Southern side, joining pro-Confederate guerrillas known as 'bushwhackers'. Led by 'Bloody' Bill Anderson, the group gained a reputation for brutality against their Unionist opponents. In 1864 Jesse James himself killed the leader of a Union force sent to intercept the guerrillas at Centralia, Missouri. This moved Anderson to remark with pride that Jesse was 'the cleanest and keenest fighter in the command'.

After the Confederate defeat, Jesse James made his way back to his hometown. He is said to have settled down and attended church services with his mother. But the years he had spent during the war as a roving desperado had changed him and, with a gang of outlaws, he embarked on a string of bank robberies, train holdups and stagecoach hijackings across the mid-west, which were to earn him folk hero status and a cherished reputation among the people of the South, despite the brutality of his crimes.

During a bloody career spanning seventeen years, the James boys and their cronies the Youngers (brothers Cole, Jim, John and Bob Younger) were the most feared and most wanted outlaws on the American frontier, credited with plundering at least eleven banks, a county fair, seven trains and three stagecoaches. Their activities covered at least eleven states: Missouri, Kentucky, Tennessee, Iowa, Kansas, Minnesota, Texas, Arkansas, Louisiana, Alabama, and West Virginia. A typical raid was on a bank at Gallatin, Missouri, in 1869. While his brother held the horses outside, Jesse approached a bank teller and asked him to change a $100 bill. While the man was busy counting out the notes, Jesse, in a fit of rage, shot him six times, scooped $700 from his drawer and fled 'laughing like a madman' according to eyewitnesses. He later told friends that the clerk resembled a Union officer who, towards the end of the Civil War, had killed his comrade in arms, 'Bloody' Bill Anderson.

After a raid in Kansas City in 1872, a letter believed to be from Jesse was received by a local newspaper. Referring to the approaching presidential election, it read: 'Just let a party of men commit a bold robbery, and the cry is hang them. But [Unionist President Ulysses S.] Grant and his party can steal millions and it is all right. They rob the poor and rich, and we rob the rich and give to the poor.' The brutality of his crimes would seem conclusive proof that Jesse James was something very different from a philanthropic 'Robin Hood'. But his cult status among the impoverished settlers and farmers of the South, still reeling from the bitter humiliation of defeat, continued to grow. To them, he was indeed a cavalier figure, a swashbuckling hero of the war because of the daring guerrilla raids in which he had taken part. His reputation was further boosted because his victims were the two institutions of the day most hated by the populace: the railroads, which ran through their prime cropland, and the banks, which owned most of their property.

Jesse would openly stroll around towns such as Nashville and Kansas City and on one occasion even bought a drink for a Pinkerton Agency detective hunting him. The detective confided that his ultimate wish was to confront James. Later he received a note from his quarry: 'Go head and die – you've seen Jesse James.' Jesse loved playing to the crowd. During a Missouri train holdup he presented the guard with his latest press cuttings.

The James-Younger Gang dissolved in 1876 following the capture of the Younger brothers in a botched bank raid at Northfield, Minnesota, during which a cashier who refused to open the vault was shot dead. The enraged townsfolk took up arms and, in the subsequent gunfight, two of the raiders were killed and every one of the remainder of the gang wounded, including Jesse who was shot in the thigh while escaping. The famous fugitive survived, however, and recruited new gang members to launch a new string of railroad robberies.

The cult status of Jesse James was finally and firmly forged upon his death. The outlaw, then aged 34 and living under the alias 'Mr Howard', was shot dead in 1882 by a member of his own gang, Bob Ford, whose brother Charley was an accomplice to the slaying. According to folklore, the Ford brothers had arrived at Jesse's home in St Joseph, Missouri, supposedly to plan another robbery. The real motive for their visit, however, was to claim a reward and a pardon from the authorities. During their meeting, Jesse noticed that the framed inscription, 'God Bless This House' was crooked. He stood on a chair to straighten it – and was shot in the back of the head.

The cold-blooded slaying made headlines across the nation. Robert Ford applied for his reward to Missouri Governor Thomas Theodore Crittenden, a man who had publicly praised James's heroism during the bloody Civil War. Instead, within a single day, Ford was charged with first-degree murder, indicted, pleaded guilty, sentenced to hang, then granted a full pardon. The deal caused public sympathy for the murdered renegade to soar further. James's mother Zerelda wrote his headstone epitaph: 'In Loving Memory of my Beloved Son, Murdered by a Traitor and Coward Whose Name is not Worthy to Appear Here.' Meanwhile, the owner of the house in which Jesse James died chopped up the floor and sold the blood-stained souvenirs for a dollar a time.

Henry Plummer looked like the answer to every law-abiding citizen's prayers. A black-bearded giant of a man, he was running for sheriff of Bannack, Montana, on a law-and-order platform in the spring of 1863, promising his voters an escape-proof jail and the tallest gallows in the country. More than that, he told the frightened gold miners who made up most of his constituents that his special target would be 'The Innocents', a gang of cut-throats who had terrorised the goldfields for two years. Men who had reaped a fortune on their claims had not survived to enjoy it. With a death toll of more than 120 citizens on the trails out of Bannack and Virginia City, nobody dared leave either camp with a poke of gold dust on them.

When elected, Plummer's first act was to call in the carpenters. Saws were soon whining and hammers resounding as his new gallows took shape. Next he deputised three hard-faced gunfighters to 'clean up' the lawless region and several arrests were quickly made. Plummer himself officiated at the first hanging. The convicted horse thief plunged to eternity in a dramatic public display and the tough sheriff's reputation as a town-tamer was established.

In the bleak badlands outside the camps, however, the Innocents continued to plunder and kill. Plummer told the disgruntled miners that he and his deputies were scouring the trails for the outlaws, who always seemed to avoid his posse. By another coincidence, the stage lines were hit when they were carrying the richest cargo. The reason, of course, was that Plummer was not only the sheriff but a ringleader of the Innocents!

Unsuspecting, the professional men of Virginia City's business community, headed by Colonel Wilbur Fisk Sanders, decided that the sheriff and his deputies needed support and formed a citizens' group called the 'Montana Vigilantes' which succeeded in rounding up several gang members of the Innocents. It was when one of them, Red Yeager, was being hauled onto the scaffold that Plummer's cover was blown. 'I don't mind dying,' Yeager shouted, 'but I'd like to have company! The boss of this gang is your sheriff, Hank Plummer.' It was the turn of Bannack's law-and-order sheriff to face his own gallows. Between December 1863 and February 1864, the vigilante committee executed Plummer and twenty-two fellow members of the Innocents.

If Henry Plummer sounds to be the crookedest sheriff who ever strode the Wild West, it must be remembered that the 'good guys' were often worse than the 'bad guys' and that the long arm of the law was often as bent as a saloon-bar fiddler's elbow!

In fact, one of the most lawless lawmen of all time was a former saloon keeper, gambler, Civil War guerrilla and smuggler named Roy Bean. Backed by the Texas Rangers, 56-year-old Bean won the job of judge of the town of Vinegaroon in 1892 – because he had picked up a smattering of law from fellow poker players. What laws Judge Bean did not know, however, he would make up. He would fine people and pocket the cash. On other occasions, he would stop trials to play a few hands of poker with the accused and to serve liquor to jurors, lawyers and even the defendant.

Bean also doubled as Vinegaroon's coroner. When a local fell 300ft to his death, Bean searched the body and found $40 and a revolver. Obviously considering the coroner's $5 fee to be insufficient, he announced: 'I find this corpse guilty of carrying a concealed weapon and I fine it $40.'

Another Civil War renegade was Wild Bill Hickok. The former Union scout, whose real name was James Butler Hickok, turned to gambling at the cessation of hostilities and once shot dead a fellow card sharp and cheat. On the basis of his reputation as a gunslinger – highly elaborated upon, no doubt – Hickok was given the job of marshal of Abilene, Kansas. His career as a lawman got off to an inauspicious start when he had to tackle a party of roistering drunks. He shot wildly into the mob and killed one of his own deputies.

Hickok became a popular public character when he joined Buffalo Bill's travelling stage show, demonstrating his supposed prowess with the six-shooter and telling terrible lies about his days as a lawman. With the money he earned, Hickok went on a wild spree of gambling, boozing and whoring. In 1876, at the age of 39, he was shot in the back during a poker game in Deadwood, South Dakota. When he died, Wild Bill was holding a pair of aces and eights, a series of cards that became known around the world as the Dead Man's Hand.

Buffalo Bill was not much better than his protege Hickok. Born William Frederick Cody in Iowa in 1846, he became a cowboy, Indian fighter, scout, buffalo shooter and Pony Express rider. But he found his true role in life as a showman. While on a drinking spree in North Platte, Nebraska, he was affronted to discover that no festivities had been planned for the Fourth of July, so he spontaneously advertised a talent show, urging local cowboys to show off their skills. He expected no more than 100 volunteers but more than 1,000 turned up.

Calling himself Buffalo Bill, the instant entrepreneur took his Wild West show on tour. It was still running thirty years later, having visited every large town in the West, as well as wowing Broadway and touring Europe. When the show reached London, Queen Victoria was awed by tales of his mythical exploits. The boastful liar was encouraged in his wild claims by a series of over 100 dime novels, packed with stories of gunfights and heroism that never happened. Buffalo Bill made a fortune during his stage days but gambled and drank away all of it. He died broke in 1917.

Another 'hero' whose reputation was built by works of fiction was Wyatt Earp. The myth that created this most famous 'good guy' of the badlands was hatched by author Stuart Lake, who sold a story to the *Saturday Evening Post* in praise of the 'bravest lawman' in the West.

In truth, Earp, born in 1848, was only briefly a lawman and it is doubtful he ever became marshal of Dodge City or Tombstone, where his legendary exploits are reputed to have taken place. Earp did take the job of marshal of Lamar, Missouri, but only briefly; he soon decided that hunting buffalo in Kansas was more lucrative. He returned to police work in Wichita but spent every day and night gambling and was thrown out of town.

That is how Wyatt Earp came to Dodge City and to fall in with one of the West's most misrepresented characters, John Henry 'Doc' Holliday. Far from being a kindly doctor with a mission to aid the sick, Holliday was a Baltimore alcoholic with minor qualifications in dentistry. Although tubercular and a virtual walking skeleton, he had a violent temper and gunned down fourteen men in his extraordinary career.

Wyatt Earp teamed up with Holliday and a fellow rogue, Bat Masterson. Masterson was sheriff of Ford County and Earp became assistant marshal of Dodge City, although that did not prevent them all from enjoying a life of boozing and womanising. It was not long before Earp was again thrown out of town and, along with his brothers and Doc Holliday, they arrived in Tombstone, Arizona, in 1879, intent on making their fortunes by fair means or foul.

Wyatt worked for Wells Fargo before being given the job of keeping the peace in one of Tombstone's dens of gambling and vice. Although today he would be known as no more than a 'bouncer', Earp managed to install his cronies as croupiers. The gang's fortunes flourished, particularly after Wyatt's brother Virgil took over the job of acting marshal following the untimely death of the holder of that office.

Bat Masterson had remained one of Earp's associates and was recruited in 1881 to lead a posse in pursuit of raiders who had held up the Tombstone stage. They returned empty handed ... not surprisingly, since it was rumoured that the holdup had been masterminded by Earp, Masterson and Holliday, with the help of the notorious Clanton gang. When later that year Earp had his famous shoot-out with the Clantons in the Gunfight at the OK Corral, he made sure that not a single Clanton was left alive to point a finger at him.

The gunfight in Tombstone lasted only thirty seconds, with thirty bullets being fired, and was not even at the OK Corral but in nearby Fremont Street. But it came to represent a period of the Old West when the frontier was still an open range across which outlaws roamed until checked by fearless and honest lawmen. Wyatt Earp was hardly that. In fact, he was not the central figure in the shoot-out, because his far more experienced brother Virgil was Tombstone's marshal that day. Perhaps that's the reason why the ignoble gunman moved quietly on, quitting Tombstone to run bars in Nevada and Alaska.

Wyatt Earp sank into relative obscurity, eventually dying in Los Angeles at the age of 80 in 1929. Only after his death did Stuart Lake write the biography, *Wyatt Earp: Frontier Marshal*, that immortalised the bent lawman as a hero of the Wild West. It was the romantic picture of cowboys, with white hats and codes of honour, that the world seemed to want. Which is why books, comics, movies and television series have depicted some of the West's worst 'baddies' as being the most valiant lawmakers who ever reached for their guns.

So much for the 'heroes'. What of the 'heroines' of the West? If the rootin' tootin' tough guys of the American frontier played rough, then their gals were often even rougher. Far from being the fairer sex, most of the Wild West's most infamous gunwomen were as ugly as they were sinful. Unlike Hollywood's portrayal of them as sexy, well-mannered ladies with tiny guns concealed in their cleavages, they were in reality tough, cut-throat outlaws with all the grace of stampeding elephants. It was not uncommon for them to take a man to bed and days later gun him down. They had names such as Madame Moustache, Big Nose Kate, Calamity Jane, China Mary, Poker Alice and Belle Starr (who looked more like Ringo Starr than a belle).

Poker Alice (real name Alice Ivers) was the daughter of an English schoolteacher. But no scholarly pursuits for her – she spent most of her time gambling at cards. She smoked huge cigars, wore outrageously expensive clothes and, when her husband died, she opened a whorehouse. She is known to have killed at least two men. But like most gamblers she ended up losing all her money. In 1930 she died destitute at the age of 79.

Kate Fisher, or Big Nose Kate as she was known because of her startling protuberance, was a dancing girl who joined up with Wyatt Earp's gang and became Doc Holliday's girlfriend. As well as being an alcoholic, a gambler, a killer and a tuberculosis sufferer, Doc Holliday must also have been severely myopic, for Big Nose Kate was possibly the ugliest of all the women in the Wild West.

Calamity Jane, born Martha Jane Cannary, lived on a diet of chewing tobacco, liquor, swearing, cursing and fighting. She skinned mules, scouted for the US Army, served under General Custer and fell in love with the alcoholic gambler Wild Bill Hickok. Hickok was shot in the back during a poker game in 1876 and Jane was buried near her lover when she died a quarter of a century later in 1903.

Other Wild West women lived equally brutal lives. Madame Moustache, China Mary, Blonde Marie and Dutch Annie were whorehouse madams in brothels dotted across the West. Life was tough, the men were rough and drinking and gambling were the amusements enjoyed by the girls when they weren't otherwise entertaining their clients. One, Pauline Cushman, was at least presentable. A former actress, her San Francisco music hall act drove men wild as she fired six guns into the ceiling. In her later years as a bar-room predator, she would goad suitors to have gunfights over her and then sleep with the winner.

Belle Starr was an outlaw who also seemed to bring bullets raining down upon every man with whom she slept. Born to a Dallas horse breeder in 1848, she married a Native American called Sam Starr and both spent time in jail for horse stealing. Belle had affairs with countless men. She fell in love with and had the child of Cole Younger, a member of Jesse James's gang who was eventually jailed for life after a bank shoot-out. Belle also had affairs with John Middleton and Indian Blue Duck, both of whom were shot dead by Sam

Above: 'Agent Zigzag'… Eddie Chapman's police mugshots from the 1930s before the cool crook became a master of espionage and an unlikely hero to both Britain and Nazi Germany.

Below: The spy who loved me… Eddie Chapman had mistresses galore but was married to Betty Farmer for fifty years.

Above left: The Greatest Showman… Phineas Taylor Barnum (pictured with his most famous exhibit Tom Thumb) believed: 'There's a sucker born every minute.'

Above right: Hot gospeller… Jim Bakker urged his TV congregations to follow God's ways, despite salting away an illicit fortune and cheating on his wife Tammy.

Below left: Hot sex… Bakker took church secretary Jessica Hahn to a hotel room for a drug-fuelled romp before kneeling for a moment of prayer.

Below right: Catch Me If You Can… Frank Abagnale inspired the movie of that title, in which his most infamous exploit was passing himself off as an airline pilot.

The Scottish 'laird'… Villagers believed that
Anthony Williams was a wealthy aristocrat but
his money was milked from his employers,
London's police service!

Above left, above right and right: Missing
masterpiece… Brazen burglars stole the
Mona Lisa from The Louvre, Paris. By the
time it was returned, Vincenzo Peruggia and
his gang had 'mass-produced' forgeries of the
priceless painting.

Above left and above right: Missing missionary… Lovelorn Joyce McKinney accused of kidnapping a young Mormon and holding him for days as an unwilling sex slave.

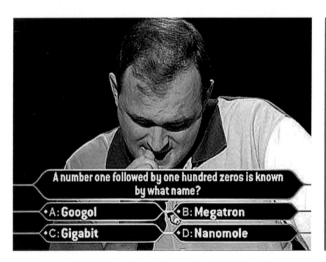

Above left: Cheating major… British TV quiz entrant Charles Ingram fleetingly got his hands on a cheque for £1million before it was snatched back.

Above right: Quiz king… Charles Van Doren gained fame on America's top TV quiz show until he was exposed as a cheat.

Wily wizard of Oz… Peter Foster could lay claim to the inglorious title 'World's Greatest Living Conman' because of his lifetime of scams.

Embarrassing liaison … Ever the charmer, Peter Foster used his lover Carole Caplin (right) to gain the trust of her friend, Prime Minister's wife Cherie Blair.

Above and opposite: Butch Cassidy and the Sundance Kid… Almost as handsome as depicted in the movie, these are the real faces of Butch (left) and Sundance with wife Etta Place.

Above left and above right: Hitler's dodgy diaries... The 'private papers' of the Führer were about to be published worldwide until they were exposed as blatant forgeries.

Above left: All that glitters... Prospectors Philip Arnold and John Slack 'seeded' the wilderness with worthless stones to dupe a bank into diamond fever.

Above right: The vanishing skyjacker... The mysterious 'D.B. Cooper' took a flight to nowhere – and parachuted out with $200,000.

VIP vanishing act… Politician John Stonehouse not only swapped his identity but also his wife – for sultry secretary, Sheila Buckley. Here they are pictured together after his release from prison.

Above left: The art of fakery… Tom Keating exposed the phoney values of the art world by painting hundreds of fakes – or 'Sexton Blakes' as he called them in Cockney rhyming slang.

Above right: Art of deception… John Myatt helped perpetrate what was described as 'the biggest art fraud of the twentieth century'.

Hailed a hero… But Han van Meegeren's forgeries almost got him hanged as a traitor because he had sold them to the Nazis.

Above left: Prison cell entrepreneur… Daniel Faries is interviewed on TV after his lucrative business behind bars was exposed.

Above right: The boss's office… Cell 10 B3 of Miami-Dade County Prison, HQ of the 'Jailhouse Shopping Co'.

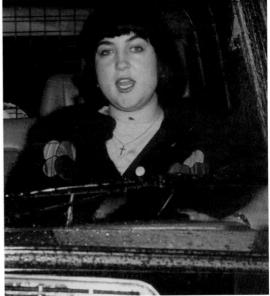

Above left: Custodian of the locked chest… Washerwoman Thérèse Humbert funded a lavish lifestyle on the promise of a non-existent inheritance.

Above right: Living on charity… Self-styled 'Lady' Rosemary Aberdour blew a fortune on luxury homes, lavish parties, flash cars and designer jewellery.

Above left and above right: Big fat phoney… Arthur Orton was an obese, coarse, semi-literate butcher, yet claimed to be the long-lost heir of one of Britain's most aristocratic families.

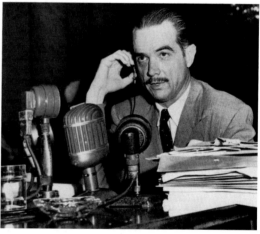

Above and left: Work of fiction… Clifford Irving (pictured with wife Edith) sold the publishing coup of the century, the 'authorised biography' of billionaire Howard Hughes (*right*) – even though he'd never even met the reclusive tycoon.

Right and below:
Runaway robber…
Ronnie Biggs in a
police picture after the
Great Train Robbery
and years later in Rio
de Janeiro during his
rip-roaring life on
the run.

Lying through the lens… William Mumler, the original exponent of so-called 'spirit photography', convinced his customers that he could capture images of the dead.

Madam Cyn… A two-fingered salute from Cynthia Payne, the whip-wielding madam whose bawdy house parties attracted vicars, lawyers, peers and politicians.

The 'Bouncing Czech'…
'Count' Victor Lustig (pictured
above, under arrest) was among
the most audacious confidence
tricksters of all time – his
greatest coup being the sale of
Paris's Eiffel Tower.

Landmark cases…
Monumental coups of
the kings of con-trickery
included the sale of
New York's Statue of
Liberty and London's
Big Ben clock tower.

Starr. Her other lovers included a brigand called Jim Reed, who was killed, and another Native American called Jim July. Sam Starr himself died by the gun – as did Belle, who was shot in the back while riding her horse in 1889.

By contrast (and to show that not all Wild West's gals were ghastly), Annie Oakley, who inspired the musical *Annie Get Your Gun*, is a more honourable example of the frontier female. Born Phoebe Mosey on a dirt farm in Ohio in 1860, she developed hunting skills as a child in order to provide for her impoverished family. She changed her name supposedly in recognition of a kindly Mr Oakley who paid her train fare when she was travelling between ranches begging for work. From those humble beginnings, the 5ft tall phenomenon became so famous that she performed for European heads of state including Queen Victoria and Kaiser Wilhelm II, for whom she shot the ash off his cigarette.

Annie was a virtuoso with a rifle. She would practise her target skills by shooting the heart out of a playing card. She used to shoot apples off the top of her pet dog's head or hit a dime coin while holding her rifle backwards over her shoulder and aiming through the reflection of the blade of her knife. She could shoot cigarettes out of people's mouths at a distance of 30 yards.

At the age of 15, Annie supported herself by shooting game for a hotel in Cincinnati. Then one day America's most famous rifleman, Frank Butler, rode into town and offered a prize of $50 to anyone who could beat him. The diminutive teen was laughed at when she accepted the challenge but she outshot him – not only winning the prize money but Butler's heart, with the couple marrying a year later.

When the pair got the offer to work together in Buffalo Bill's Wild West travelling show, it was Annie who was the star and Frank his wife's assistant. They last performed in the show in 1901. On the journey home their train was involved in a head-on collision and Annie was so badly injured that despite having numerous operations she was never able to walk properly again. In 1916 she was involved in another accident, this time in a car. Doctors told her she would never walk again, let alone shoot a rifle, but she proved them wrong by appearing once more before an audience, shooting all twenty-five coins that were thrown in the air for her.

In 1926 Annie died of anaemia, in Greenville, Ohio, leaving in her will more than £100,000, a fabulous sum in those days. Three weeks later Frank Butler died, it is said of grief for the woman who epitomised to the world the fiery spirit of the Wild West.

Konrad Kujau
Author of Hitler's Dodgy Diaries

It was an insight into the mind of one of the most evil dictators in history: the man who wanted to change the world, the man responsible for millions of deaths and the man whose name today still conjures up as much fear and loathing. The earth-shattering discovery was a collection of the private diaries of Adolf Hitler. They had never been seen before. And written between 1932 and 1945, they spanned a watershed in world history.

First to study these intimate revelations was the German news magazine *Stern* which, already envisaging a circulation rise to record figures, was fully prepared to pay the equivalent of £2.5million for the exclusive rights to the documents. Other prestigious publications were to follow: *Paris Match, Newsweek* and even Britain's august newspaper *The Sunday Times*. But in handing over small fortunes for Der Führer's diaries, they were paying the price of being too hungry and too hasty for a scoop.

The diaries were fakes – and, as was later revealed, not even clever fakes. The handwriting was unlike Hitler's, the paper was dodgy, the ink was new and the bindings were of a type not produced until ten years after the dictator's death. And yet the fraudsters who created and marketed them succeeded in fooling hard-bitten newspaper executives and historical experts.

It was 1983 when *Stern* and *The Sunday Times* announced the existence of several volumes of Hitler's wartime jottings. No one had any reason to suspect they had been penned by a devious trickster who had teamed up with a chancer down on his luck. Front man in the scam was Gerd Heidemann, a 53-year-old award-winning journalist employed by a reputable magazine – none other than *Stern*. The forger was Konrad 'Konni' Kujau, 46, erstwhile waiter and talented artist with a fertile imagination.

Kujau was born in 1938 in the Saxon town of Löbau which at that time was enjoying the prosperity of Hitler's Third Reich. From 1946 to 1991, however, it became part of East Germany and Kujau fled to the West in 1957 to avoid arrest following petty theft whilst employed waiting tables. He settled in Stuttgart and changed his name to Peter Fischer, but this didn't stop him getting into more trouble, and further minor misdemeanours led to two prison sentences. He opened the Pelican Dance Bar in 1962, going into business with Edith Lieblang, a waitress and fellow refugee, but when this failed he returned to work as a waiter. Kujau was evidently set in his criminal ways, however, and before long was in prison once more, this time for forging luncheon vouchers. Edith stuck by him and, after his release, Kujau persuaded her to put up the money for The Lieblang Cleaning Company. The business prospered and their happiness was marred only by another spell in jail when the authorities discovered 'Peter Fischer' was not who he said he was.

A visit back home to Löbau gave Kujau a money-making idea. It was now twenty-five years since Hitler's death but there was a growing market for Nazi memorabilia. Kujau got his family to place adverts in East German newspapers. They read: 'Wanted for research; old toys, helmets, jugs, pipes, dolls etc.' The response was great and although the East German government had banned the export of objects made before 1945, Kujau managed to smuggle many into West Germany. He now supplemented his living by selling these relics from a shop in Stuttgart's Aspergstrasse.

Kujau never missed a chance to pull a fast one on eager collectors, cashing in on their craving for historical material, and he was not above manufacturing his own certificates of authenticity. For instance, a note authenticating a helmet as being worn by Adolf Hitler in 1917 was signed by Rudolf Hess. Kujau 'aged' documents by soaking them in tea – a technique well-learned, for it was to stand him in good stead when the great Hitler Diaries Hoax was conceived.

Kujau moved on to the art world, specialising in the supposedly original works of Adolf Hitler himself. This business venture was to lead to his relationship with another keen collector of Nazi memorabilia, Fritz Stiefel. A wealthy owner of a local engineering works, Stiefel was an avid collector of militaria. Over a period of six years, Stiefel spent large sums of money at Kujau's store, for the shopkeeper seemed to have a never-ending supply of prized Nazi items. There were 160 drawings, oil paintings and watercolours by Hitler himself, as well as poems, notes of speeches and letters. Their manufacture kept Kujau very busy. Poor Stiefel never suspected a thing.

Kujau decided that Stiefel deserved a real gem as a reward for his faithful custom. He would be offered a diary written in the Führer's own hand. It was now 1980 and news of the startling find soon reached the ears of *Stern* journalist Gerd Heidemann, who was also obsessed with the Third Reich. Indeed, his wife had left him when their apartment was taken over by Heidemann's collection of war games and toy soldiers. The purchase of Hermann Goering's old motor yacht, plus a string of love affairs, had left Heidemann heavily in debt, and he clearly saw the financial potential of Hitler's diaries.

Heidemann opened negotiations with Fritz Stiefel who, although refusing to name Kujau, was nevertheless happy to act as an intermediary. When he told Heidemann there could be as many as twenty-six volumes of the diaries, a deal was swiftly struck. Heidemann never doubted the authenticity of the new discovery, and his enthusiasm seems to have become infective. Thomas Walde, editor of the historical department at *Stern,* became involved in the negotiations. As any experienced reporter would do, he had embarked on background research and learned, to his great excitement, that on 20 April 1945, close to the end of the Second World War, a courier aircraft had crashed near the Czechoslovakian border. The plane had been carrying Hitler's personal papers to his retreat near Berchtesgaden. Heidemann concluded the diaries must have been among them.

Heidemann and Walde decided not to approach *Stern's* editor Peter Koch with their incredible news because Koch had repeatedly told Heidemann to drop his Nazi obsessions. The two men instead took the first of Hitler's diaries and their background information to senior executives of the publishing house Gruner and Jahr, the owners of *Stern.* A total payment was agreed. It was to be made in instalments as and when the diaries were received.

Kujau began his work in earnest. He compiled the diaries drawing on his huge reference library. They bore a red wax seal of a German eagle. Heidemann was the go-between and no one at Gruner and Jahr was aware that from every instalment of cash they gave him to pay to Kujau, Heidemann creamed off a cut for himself. The collation of the Hitler Diaries took two years. Crafty Kujau – still going under the alias Herr Fischer – insisted he could only pass on the books when they arrived in his hands from his contacts in East Germany. Kujau, of course, needed a fair amount of time between 'consignments' to write them from scratch.

Each time Herr Fischer insisted it was getting increasingly difficult to obtain the diaries, he was offered more and more money. It was no wonder that by 1983, the year of publication, *Stern* had paid £2.5million. Yet it seems incredible now that *Stern* and a host of eminent academics could have been taken in by the often childlike nature of the entries. Here are some of them:

> Ten thousand Communists meet in Berlin Sports Palace, pledge
> will fight fascism to last breath. Demonstration, many arrests. By
> Jove, we must stamp out the reds.

> Meet all the leaders of the stormtroopers in Bavaria, give them
> medals. They pledge lifelong loyalty to the Fuhrer, with tears in
> their eyes. What a splendid body of men!

Of the famous bomb plot against Hitler by the German generals, Kujau recorded gleefully:

> Ha! Ha! Isn't it laughable? These people were bunglers. This scum, these loafers and good-for-nothings!

Three experts who examined the handwriting before publication of the diaries agreed it was indeed that of Adolf Hitler. The verdict from a police expert that some of the paper in the diaries was not in use until after the war was somehow lost in the excitement as *Stern's* momentous publication day drew near. Meanwhile, *The Sunday Times* offered $3.25million for the English language rights and *Newsweek* offered $3million for American rights. As its big day, 3 May 1993, came closer, *Stern* demanded $4.25million from both publications. But it had overplayed its hand. The asking price was too much and, sadly for *Stern, Newsweek* had already secured enough of Hitler's Diaries to go ahead and publish anyway. *Stern* retaliated by changing its publication date to 25 April. It wooed *The Sunday Times* back into a deal by accepting $1.2million for the diaries, and it was planned that the great British newspaper would announce its scoop on 24 April.

Stern, Newsweek, Paris Match and *The Sunday Times* had now all bought the rights in good faith and started to publish extracts. In their 'scoops', they explained that Heidemann had managed to obtain the historic material from East German contacts. The papers had been discovered in a hay loft where they had supposedly been hidden after the plane crash.

One correspondent was certainly fooled by what he read in *The Sunday Times*. In its fellow newspaper *The Times*, Frank Johnson wrote:

> At least when *The Sunday Times* published its first extract, your present correspondent, a lifelong amateur student of mid-twentieth-century European politics, had no doubt that the diaries were genuine; they were so boring. Hitler exerts his fascination with his deeds rather than his prose. On that Sunday, those of us familiar with *Mein Kampf*, the *Collected Speeches* and *Table Talk*, knew that this was the authentic voice.

However, new forensic evidence was being produced that appeared to prove the diaries were fake. Experts at the Federal Archives in Koblenz were finally allowed to examine some of the writings – and declared them obvious forgeries, produced on post-war paper. One detail that proved the diaries were fraudulent was the result of Kujau's over-confidence, resulting in him making a ludicrous blunder. When he bought the Gothic letters in Hong Kong to stick on the diary covers, he mixed up the letters 'A' and 'F'. Adorning the volumes were the imitation metal initials 'FH' instead of 'AH'!

Kujau and Heidemann were arrested in May 1983. Heidemann, his record as a star writer ruined forever, was charged with defrauding the magazine. He maintained throughout the eleven-month trial in Hamburg that he had believed the diaries to be genuine and told the court that Kujau had also offered him an unpublished volume of Hitler's autobiography *Mein Kampf*. He said: 'When I heard the diaries were fakes, I wondered whether to shoot myself then or later.'

The extent of Heidemann's obsession with Hitler was revealed after German police raided his home. They took photographs of objects which had once adorned Hitler's desk, including a swastika on a red background which Heidemann said was Hitler's 'martyr's flag'. Heidemann also had in his bizarre collection a pair of underpants that had once belonged to Idi Amin.

Kujau was charged with forgery. He pleaded guilty and appeared to bask in the attention he attracted during the court proceedings. In his defence, Kujau said he at first intended to write only three diaries in return for a uniform worn by Hermann Goering which Heidemann had shown him. 'I had to have it,' he told the court. He said he had forged one Hitler diary in 1978 because it annoyed him that the Fuhrer had apparently left no records of his life.

Kujau claimed Heidemann had first told him he wanted to discuss the diaries so that they could be sent to Martin Bormann, Hitler's former deputy, in South America. He told the court: 'Heidemann said the diaries would help to rehabilitate Bormann but I began to doubt the story. Then in January 1982, Heidemann told me Bormann was seriously ill and I should hurry my work.' Kujau, who admitted the forgeries had earned him £415,000, said he was sure Heidemann had rumbled his trickery after he had practised writing the word 'helmet' in Hitler's script on a piece of paper which the journalist had spotted. But an indication of Heidemann's gullibility came soon afterwards in Kujau's evidence. Court observers couldn't help but snigger when they heard that Kujau had once provided the obsessed journalist with fake ashes of Hitler, supplied by a friend who worked in a crematorium.

The prosecution's case against the forgers filled 4,000 pages and involved sixty-two witnesses and eight experts. Eminent historian Lord Dacre of Glanton (otherwise known as Hugh Trevor-Roper, author of *The Last Days of Hitler*) who had at first declared the diaries to be genuine, had the courage to admit his mistake. He expressed this doubt at a conference in Hamburg in April 1983, called by increasingly concerned executives of *Stern*. He also said he had tried to warn *The Sunday Times*.

As the trial dragged on, fascinating evidence was heard, producing copy as riveting as the fake diaries themselves. A German professor, Eberhard Jäckel, had published some of Kujau's earlier work before the big scandal broke – and said that experts had seen through them straight away. *Sunday Times* writer Gita Sereny said she had been dispatched to Germany after a tip-off about the diaries but had not been allowed to consult Jäckel because of the extra cost it would have involved. The court also heard that *Stern* executives had given a page of the diaries to experts to study, without explaining why. The experts they had engaged did not know what they were looking for and passed the copies as authentic. This meant the ink and tea-soaked paper used for the diaries had not been tested until it was too late.

On 8 July 1985, Heidemann and Kujau were both found guilty. Heidemann was jailed for four years and eight months. His friends said he had been used as a scapegoat by *Stern,* whose weekly circulation dropped by 100,000 when the deception was announced. Kujau was sent to jail for four years and six months. His faithful girlfriend, Edith Lieblang, who was accused of spending part of the ill-gotten gains, was given an eight-month suspended sentence. No one found out where all the money went.

Everyone else involved in the great Hitler Diary Hoax suffered some sorry fate. Poor Thomas Walde was humiliated in court for being so gullible. *Stern* editors Peter Koch and Felix Schmidt were fired, even though they had been kept in the dark about the diary dealings. Gruner and Jahr's managing director Gerd Schulte-Hillen, who had inherited the diaries from his predecessor but had backed Heidemann, was given a severe dressing down but was allowed to stay on at *Stern.* Frank Giles, editor of *The Sunday Times*, retired to become 'editor emeritus'.

In *Selling Hitler, the Story of the Hitler Diaries,* author Richard Harris tells how Rupert Murdoch, owner of *The Sunday Times,* justified Giles's new title: 'It's Latin. The "e" means you're out and "meritus" means you deserve it!' But perhaps Harris best sums up the whole scam with the following anecdote. Murdoch, who ordered *The Sunday Times* to continue printing even when told Lord Dacre was sounding the alarm, did so with the words: 'After all, we're in the entertainment business!'

Philip Arnold and John Slack
'All That Glitters...'

Phoney 'discoveries' of precious metals and gems were common in the years following the California Gold Rush of 1849. Tricksters fooled many innocents by 'salting' worthless mines with particles of gold, silver and even diamonds. That didn't stop the fortune hunters from flooding in. From grubby prospectors to city bankers and international speculators, everyone, it seemed, wanted to believe that the West's waterbeds and mountains held untold riches. And thus the stage was set for the Great Diamond Hoax, a brilliantly acted scam by two Kentucky cousins that involved some of California's biggest bankers and businessmen, a former commander of the Union Army, a US representative, leading lawyers on both coasts, and the founder of Tiffany & Co.

On a summer day in 1872, two old-timer gold prospectors, Philip Arnold and John Slack, sauntered into the Bank of California in San Francisco ready to pull off one of the cleverest confidence tricks of all time.

Philip Arnold was a poorly educated former hatter's apprentice, a Mexican War veteran and Gold Rush 'Forty-Niner', who had spent twenty years working in mining operations in the West, making enough money to pay for visits back to Kentucky, where he bought a farm, got married and had a family. In 1870, he was working as an assistant bookkeeper for the Diamond Drill Company, a San Francisco drill maker that used diamond-headed bits. For a bookkeeper, Arnold, then aged just over 40, showed a surprising interest in the industrial-grade diamonds that kept the drills running. By November that year, Arnold had acquired a bag of uncut diamonds which he mixed with garnets, rubies and sapphires. By now, he also had as his partner John Slack, an older cousin from Kentucky who, like Arnold, had fought in the Mexican War and had gone after gold in 1849.

As the grizzled fraudsters walked through the doors of the Bank of California, Arnold and Slack had every reason to feel happy with life for, as a greedy bank teller was to discover, they were bearing a wonderful hoard. The two men slammed a drawstring sack on the counter and demanded that it be kept in the bank's safe. Satisfied that their 'deposit' was in safe keeping, the two prospectors then wandered off to find a saloon in which to celebrate their good fortune. Watching all this was a teller with a strong feeling that here was a chance to cash in.

As soon as Arnold and Slack were out of sight, the teller peeked into the sack. He was expecting to see a handful or two of gold. Instead his eyes focused on more stunning, sparkling uncut diamonds than he had ever seen in his life. The startled teller picked the bag up and ran into the office of bank boss William Ralston, who had become wealthy through dubious deals but was always on the lookout for fresh ways of increasing his fortune. After examining the diamonds, he now had visions of becoming America's 'Diamond King'.

Promising the teller a suitable reward for his troubles, Ralston told him to seek out the two prospectors straight away. Ralston himself joined in the search. It took three anxious days before the prospectors were tracked down. Arnold and Slack were extremely drunk and wanted only to drink more. They could not understand what Ralston wanted with them. Conversely, Ralston could not understand their slurred words, so had to wait patiently for them to sober up.

After much coaxing, and with Ralston's promise of financial backing, Arnold and Slack eventually told the bank chief that they had found a diamond field 'bigger than Kimberley'. But they had not acquired title to the land yet and so refused to tell him exactly where it was. They would, however, allow anyone who wanted to see the diamond field to do so – as long as their visitor made the entire journey blindfolded. Ralston, his imagination swimming with diamonds in unbelievable quantities, agreed. He didn't fancy making the journey himself and instead sent mining engineer David Colton, who on his return thrust a fistful of diamonds under Ralston's nose. A deal was struck. Assuming he was dealing with unsophisticated country bumpkins, Ralston already had it in his mind to take control of the diamond mine.

The banker paid Arnold and Slack $50,000, put another $300,000 aside for any expenses incurred, and pledged them a further $350,000 when they started producing their promised harvest of diamonds. By now, word had spread about the diamond prospectors' land. Everyone wanted to be part of the scheme. Joining forces with a number of other prominent San Francisco financiers, Ralston formed the New York Mining and Commercial Company, capitalised at $10million, and began selling stock to eager investors. Convinced that the American West must have many other major deposits of diamonds, at least another twenty-five diamond exploration companies were formed in the subsequent months. Those who contributed money included Baronet Anthony de Rothschild, the *New York Tribune* editor Horace Greeley, General George B. McClellan and Charles Lewis Tiffany, founder of the world's largest jewellery business.

To ensure that there was nothing untoward about what David Colton had claimed to have seen, Ralston sent along a group of witnesses to the site of Arnold and Slack's discovery. The group included an independent expert, respected mining engineer Henry Janin, who was chosen by the San Francisco investors. Cold weather meant Janin could not visit the fields until June. Arnold and Slack met up with him and a team of other Ralston representatives, and the group boarded a Union Pacific train to Rawlins, Wyoming.

Though the spot that Arnold had picked to 'salt' was closer to the Black Buttes, Wyoming, the two tricksters wanted to keep the exact location secret, so led the blindfolded party on a confusing four-day horseback journey, often pretending to be lost and climbing hills to get their bearings. When their blindfolds were removed, the visitors felt like they were dreaming. Ant hills in the valley shimmered and sparkled with diamond dust. Not only that, diamonds as big as a man's thumb and other gems were scattered across the earth.

In retrospect, what the group found was laughable. One commented later: 'He held up something glittering in his hand. For more than an hour, diamonds were being found in profusion, together with occasional rubies, emeralds and sapphires. Why a few pearls weren't thrown in for good luck I have never yet been able to tell. Probably it was an oversight.'

It was when the party reported their findings back to Ralston that he decided to get rid of Arnold and Slack and have every gem for himself. He threatened the two prospectors with legal claims, saying they had no rights. He bullied them into backing down from the deal they had made with him. Apparently worn down by Ralston's harassment, Arnold and Slack agreed to accept $700,000 for their share of the diamond field. They were then told to leave town.

News of the diamond 'Klondike' soon spread around the world. But what finally led to the hoax's collapse was an encounter on an Oakland-bound train between Janin and members of a government survey team led by Clarence King, a Yale-educated geologist. King had come West in 1863 at the age of 21, travelling by wagon train with a friend and joining the California Geological Survey. By the early 1870s, he and the three dozen men under his command had surveyed, mapped and described the whole immense patch of the West within their domain, and the fieldwork for what was known as the Fortieth Parallel Survey was nearly done.

King and his team were obviously aware of the supposed diamond harvests but most of the rumoured discoveries had been in Arizona and New Mexico, outside the survey's boundaries. So it was alarming for the team to hear from Janin that a major discovery of diamonds had been found on their 'patch' – a discovery that would make them out to be less than thorough in their surveys. King and his men determined to make an urgent inspection of the diamond fields and in October 1872 travelled east by train from Oakland to Fort Bridger, Wyoming, where mules took them on the final leg of their journey.

Arriving at the supposed diamond site, King and his team began to inspect the unusual field. King uncovered a stone partially polished and definitely not natural. He noticed the field had diamonds, rubies, emeralds and sapphires in the same area and many of the gems were in places they could not have reached by any natural means. In fact, the stones were only found in ground that had quite obviously been disturbed, rubies being discovered in anthills that were surrounded by footprints. The team's subsequent report stated: 'Our explanation was that someone must have pushed in a ruby or two on the end of a stick.'

It was later revealed that Arnold and Slack had travelled to Europe and spent their life savings of $35,000 on hordes of cheap cast-off diamonds – refuse left over from gem cutting in London and Amsterdam. The duplicitous duo had increased the number of gems still further by using a lapidary tool to split each stone into pieces. Then they had scattered them around the carefully chosen site to 'salt' the ground and hoodwink their gullible investors.

When word of the hoax came out, Ralston was a laughing stock. And when the painstaking nature of the amazing con trick perpetrated by Arnold and Slack came to light, they became popular heroes. Public sympathy was very much on the side of the colluding cousins, who even managed to escape prosecution. The *San Francisco Chronicle* described the duo's scam as:

> The most gigantic and barefaced swindle of the age, the scheme being noteworthy for the manner of its unraveling and its colorful characters. Not only did it propel to prominence a geologist later befriended and admired by Theodore Roosevelt, it also gave a fed-up American public some hope that honest science could triumph, at least occasionally, over hucksterism and greed.

Ralston returned $80,000 to each of his investors but, of course, was never able to recover the rest of the money given to the perpetrators of the Great Diamond Hoax. Arnold returned to his home in Elizabethtown, Kentucky, where he founded his own bank and lived out the few remaining years of his life in luxury. He died of pneumonia in 1878 after he was wounded in a shoot-out with a rival banker. Slack apparently went to St Louis, where he owned a coffin-making company. He later moved to White Oaks, New Mexico, where he carried on his trade and lived a quiet life until making use of one of his own caskets when he died in 1896.

As for gullible Ralston, he ended up ruined, his financial empire collapsed and his dreams of owning his very own diamond field shattered.

'D. B. Cooper'
Mystery of the Missing Skyjacker

It was 24 November 1971, Thanksgiving Eve, and the man clutching a black attaché case close to his chest in the departure lounge at Portland, Oregon, attracted little attention. The airport was crammed with travellers anxious to get home to spend the holiday with their families. The quiet, middle-aged man was among 150 passengers waiting to take the 400-mile flight from Portland to Seattle, Washington.

After acquiring a ticket under the name of Dan B. Cooper, he entered the departure lounge and waited patiently behind his dark tinted glasses. Fifty minutes later he filed aboard the Northwest Airlines Boeing 727 and took his seat at the rear of the aircraft. As he settled down with the bag on his lap to enjoy the one-hour flight, he casually ordered a drink: bourbon and soda.

Shortly after take-off, he summoned flight attendant Florence Schaffner and handed her a note neatly written in capital letters with a black felt-tip pen. The exact wording is unknown because he eventually took it back but the gist of the message, as recalled by Miss Schaffner, was: 'I have a bomb with me. If I don't get $200,000 I will blow us all to bits.' As the startled stewardess hurriedly digested the dire warning, Cooper opened the bag to show her what certainly appeared to be a bomb. She could clearly identify the dynamite sticks, wiring and detonator. Cooper never took his eyes off her as he closed the bag, watched the woman walk up to the flight deck and sat back, awaiting the response.

So began the amazing saga of a 'perfect crime' which, because of its unique conclusion, captured the imagination of an entire nation. It switched public sympathy away from the forces of law and order and onto the side of the perpetrator, the man known as D. B. Cooper who passed not into infamy but folklore. In smoky North American bars, they would sing songs about him as if he were a modern-day Robin Hood. Poems were penned in his memory, T-shirts bore his name and newspaper editors were sent letters from admiring girls pledging to be his bride. The object of all this attention was a man who certainly deserved condemnation for perpetrating one of the most shocking of crimes, skyjacking. But although he threatened to kill men, women and children, he ultimately caused harm to no one, finally leaping into sub-zero temperatures – and into enduring mystery.

Within seconds of D. B. Cooper handing his demand for $200,000 to Florence Schaffner, the pilot of Northwest Flight 305 flicked a switch which broadcast a message over several frequencies that an emergency was underway. Within two minutes it had been picked up by ground control at Seattle, where a team of FBI agents, police marksmen and units of the National Guard were mobilised and placed at strategic positions.

The plane landed uneventfully at the airport, where a message from the captain announced that disembarkation would be delayed. Amid the commotion of disgruntled passengers, Cooper left his seat. Still clutching his black attaché case, he walked through the bulkhead door onto the flight deck where he confronted the pilot, co-pilot and flight engineer. 'Now gentlemen,' he said coolly, 'don't bother to look round.' There followed a tense twenty-minute dialogue with air traffic control staff and then a police chief, who asked for the release of the passengers before any bargains were struck. The man was unequivocal in his demands. The passengers would be released only after $200,000 in used dollar bills had been handed over to him – along with four parachutes.

Cooper got his way, and two FBI agents dressed as maintenance men wheeled a trolley aboard. Inside was a white sack sealed with wire. Cooper ripped it open and found to his delight the money and the parachutes he had demanded. He then relented and allowed the passengers to leave. As they filed out to buses waiting to take them to the main terminal building, they were still unaware that a man had played a ruthless game with their lives. They thought a simple air traffic delay had held them up.

When the passengers were all safely in the terminal building, Cooper moved into the second phase of his bold plan. Now captor of only the flight crew, he began making further demands of the police and airport authorities. He asked that the plane be refuelled and that flight plans be drawn up to take the aircraft to Mexico. In his exchanges with the ground staff, Cooper displayed a depth of knowledge about aircraft which indicated he was neither a crank nor a lucky amateur. This escapade had been plotted to keep it simple – brilliantly simple.

When the aircraft took off again, it was shadowed by a US Air Force fighter scrambled to track it to its final destination. Cooper seemed to sense the precautions that the authorities down below would take and, when airborne, he told Captain Bill Scott that they were to alter course. He was not to head for Mexico but to veer south east. He issued specific instructions at Scott, again indicating a deep technical knowledge of aviation. He said: 'Fly with the flaps lowered, fifteen per cent, keep the landing gear down, keep the speed below 90 metres per second, do not climb above 7,000 feet ... and open the rear door.'

The captain did some quick mental arithmetic before telling Cooper that his instructions would mean a massive leap in fuel consumption. The skyjacker replied that he could, if he wished, land in Reno, Nevada. Then he moved from the cockpit to the body of the aircraft, turning only to order the crew to keep the bulkhead door locked. As Cooper stood in the belly of the plane, there was a huge rush of air and a deafening roar as Captain Scott activated the mechanism opening the rear door, as demanded by his sole unwanted passenger.

Scott was not to know it until he landed at Reno nearly four hours later but, in the freezing night sky, shrouded by cloud and out of sight of the shadowing military plane, Cooper made his leap into the thin air. He left behind two parachutes, one intact, one in shreds. Investigators theorised later that he had ripped one apart to make a pouch for his loot that he strapped to his body. Examination of the flight's black box recorder showed a slight increase in height at the moment he jumped as the aircraft compensated for his weight and that of his ransom. This indicated that Cooper had leapt out at 8.13pm, just thirty-two minutes after leaving Seattle.

When the aircraft landed at Reno, the authorities became painfully aware that they had been duped. An FBI contingency plan to storm the aircraft was rendered worthless but they consoled themselves with the thought that the parachute jump was the one weak point in Cooper's careful plan. The skyjacker had no winter clothes, no food, and wore just lightweight shoes and a raincoat for protection. Investigators took solace in the fact that Cooper had bailed out over rocky, mountainous, deeply wooded terrain into sub-zero temperatures and dangerous wildlife, and judged there was little point in attempting an instant ground search over such hostile terrain. Aviation experts calculated that, in any case, the odds of Cooper even surviving his leap in the dark were heavily stacked against him.

For two weeks after his vanishing act, exhaustive aerial searches covering vast tracts of land went on unabated. Planes with cameras and heat-seeking sensors criss-crossed the skyways over Oregon and Washington. There was no sign of him. Army and air force personnel joined in the ground searches but of the man and his loot there was no sign. Then three weeks after the hijacking, the following letter arrived unexpectedly at the *Los Angeles Times* office:

> I am no modern-day Robin Hood. Unfortunately I have only fourteen months left to live. The hijacking was the fastest and most profitable way of gaining a few last grains of peace. I didn't rob Northwest because I thought it would be romantic, or heroic, or any of the other euphemisms that seem to attach themselves to situations of high risk. I don't blame people for hating me for what I've done, nor do I blame anybody for wanting me caught and punished, though this can never happen. I knew from the start I would not be caught. I have come and gone on several airline flights since and I'm not holed up in some obscure backwoods town. Neither am I a psychopath. I have never received a speeding ticket.

The note, probably more than anything else, helped lift the status of D. B. Cooper from that of villain to that of folk hero. Letters poured into newspapers and radio stations across the USA praising the man who had 'beaten the system'. He might not have regarded himself as a modern-day Robin Hood but the public certainly did. A university professor was engaged by FBI agents to build up a mental profile of Cooper. His findings were never published; it is believed they would only have enhanced the glamour and mystique of the man in the eyes of the public.

Many of the 'mountain men' living in the region where Cooper jumped disregarded the letter, preferring to believe it was a spoof. Instead they embarked on wild treasure hunts amid the peaks and valleys. Clubs organised 'Cooper Loot' hunt sorties and it became fashionable for families to spend the weekends barbecuing in the mountains – with a little light treasure hunting thrown in.

The authorities harnessed the latest technology to try to trace the money or at least locate Cooper's remains. Despite the letter, many high-ranking federal agents, accepting the evidence of the experts, could not believe that he survived the leap. One year after the skyjack, the FBI publicly announced that they thought D. B. Cooper dead. Five years after the crime, on 24 November 1976, the file on him was closed and it was arguable that, under the Statute of Limitations law, even if he were alive he was a free man. The only other crime he could be convicted for was tax evasion!

In 1979 a deer hunter prowling through thick forest in Cowlitz County, south-west Washington, discovered the plastic warning sign of a Boeing 727 rear door hatch. It read: 'This hatch must remain firmly locked in flight.' The discovery was akin to gold being struck in the Klondike. Treasure-seekers from all over America poured into the nearby town of Kelso to scour the surrounding forests and mountains. In their wake came map-makers, astrologers and souvenir sellers, who certainly got richer than the luckless prospectors hunting in vain for the 'Cooper Loot'.

It was not until seven years after the crime that painter Harold Ingram and his 8-year-old son Brian made a discovery which many believe proves conclusively that Cooper died in his spectacular jump. They found $3,000 on the bank of Washington's Columbia River and experts calculated that it had probably been washed down to the tranquil picnic spot by a mountain stream. The money was identified by the serial numbers as being Cooper's haul. The Ingrams' discovery sparked a new wave of treasure fever. This time a group calling itself the 'Ransom Rangers' set out to try to find the rest of the skyjacked booty. But no more money was found, nor the remains of D. B. Cooper. 'That's the closest we ever got to him,' an FBI agent remarked of the mystery man who planned one of the strangest vanishing tricks in history.

John Stonehouse
VIP's Amazing Vanishing Act

The charming, good-looking Englishman walked casually up to the receptionist at the beachside office of Miami's luxurious Fontainebleau Hotel. Helen Fleming, a cheery 65-year-old, was happy to pass the time of day with him. Business was quiet and they were able to have a long uninterrupted conversation.

Before parting company, the well-spoken visitor mentioned that his name was John Stonehouse and that he was going for a swim. He bid her farewell and she watched as he strolled down the beach, seemingly just another Brit soaking up the Florida sunshine and surf. Hours later, his clothes were found in a neat pile on the sand. Of Mr Stonehouse there was no trace. And so began one of the most audacious deceptions of the twentieth century.

Stonehouse was a Labour Member of the British Parliament with debts of around £375,000. His business empire lay in tatters and his personal life – he was attempting to keep both a wife and mistress in tow – was a constant strain. His attempt to drag himself out of the mire by apparently vanishing off the face of the Earth was nothing short of a gigantic political scandal.

When he took his seat in the House of Commons in 1957, John Thomas Stonehouse had seemed destined for the very top. After serving his apprenticeship on the back benches he was talent spotted by Labour leader Harold Wilson and put on the fast track to promotion. During the Wilson years, he rose from aviation minister and technology minister to become postmaster general. As a privy counsellor he was entitled to be known as the Right Honourable John Stonehouse, and he was so close to the prime minister that Wilson lent him his private holiday home on the Scilly Isles. He was even tipped as the PM's successor. Not noted for modesty, Stonehouse declared to colleagues that his plan was to become a millionaire and then prime minister.

By now, however, his bumptious manner was losing him favour and when Labour lost to the Conservative Party in the 1970 elections, Stonehouse decided he could not accept either the comparative anonymity or the reduced salary of life on the House of Commons back benches. He began pumping money into a web of companies, including a merchant bank, in a bid to make his fortune. His heavily indebted business empire stretched to twenty-three separate companies. Over the next four years not one of them returned a decent profit. Stonehouse resorted to switching funds between his companies in a bid to convince investors and auditors that all was well.

In his heart, he probably knew it couldn't last, and in early 1974 he got wind that the Department of Trade's investigators were taking an interest in his heavily indebted companies. To further complicate his life, he had started an affair with his adoring secretary Sheila Buckley, which was a secret to his long-suffering wife Barbara. His glib tongue and easy charm couldn't help him now and he resolved to take desperate measures to avoid exposure. He disliked the idea of spending the rest of his life on the run so there was only one thing for it ... he would have to 'die'.

The MP shared his secret with only one person: his divorced mistress Sheila Buckley, then aged 28. The aim would be for them to move to New Zealand, living off whatever money he could smuggle out from the wreckage of his businesses. At that time, Stonehouse had debts of more than £800,000 after an attempt to set up a new investment bank in Bangladesh. He had also taken out a £170,000 insurance policy on his own life. There was only one snag: he had to have a new identity.

To 'reinvent' himself, Stonehouse used a technique described by thriller writer Frederick Forsyth in his classic *The Day of the Jackal*. He first tricked a hospital in his Walsall, Staffordshire, constituency to release personal details of two men his own age who had died recently: Donald Mildoon and Joseph Markham. The 48-year-old MP then obtained copies of their birth certificates and, believing Markham's background was closest to his own, applied for a passport in that man's name. He obtained photo-booth shots of himself wearing glasses and smiling and on the back forged the countersignature of an MP he knew to be dying of cancer, Neil McBride. The application was rubber-stamped at the passport office and on 2 August 1974, Stonehouse picked up his new passport. He now had a dual identity and could switch his name whenever necessary.

Then came the second part of his plan. Over the next three months, he opened twenty-seven accounts in his own name and a further nine in the names of Markham or Mildoon. A Swiss bank received one huge cheque credited to Mr Markham while further amounts were quietly channelled via a London account to the Bank of New South Wales. Numerous credit cards were set up in Markham's name using an anonymous address at a downmarket London hotel. He even set up a company to help his cover story: 'J. A. Markham, export-import consultant'. The only exports it handled were cash and the only customer was Stonehouse. After a dummy run to America, Stonehouse was ready for the real thing. He left London for Miami on 19 November 1974 with Jim Charlton, deputy chairman of one of his companies. When he failed to return from his swimming trip the following day, there seemed little doubt that he had drowned, perhaps by accident or possibly suicide.

The message flashed from Miami Beach Police Department to New Scotland Yard read: 'John Stonehouse Presumed Dead'. Of course, they were wrong. And the FBI were not convinced. They believed it highly unlikely that a man would drown at that stretch of the coast without a body being washed ashore. It was even suspected that the Mafia had been involved and a car park was excavated in the search for Stonehouse's remains. A body was found but it was not that of John Stonehouse. In fact, the body of Stonehouse would not be found because he was very much alive.

After dumping his clothes, the MP had raced up the beach to a ramshackle building where he had hidden a suitcase containing new clothes, cash and false identity papers. He took a taxi to the airport, flew to Hawaii via San Francisco and then called Sheila Buckley to tell her their scheme had worked like a dream. His optimism, however, was premature.

Stonehouse arrived in Australia and was soon switching cash from a bank account in Melbourne, held under the name of Mildoon, to one in New Zealand belonging to Joseph Markham. The amounts were more than enough to raise the suspicions of bank officials and the police were called. A tail was put on Stonehouse who, by 10 December, was transferring funds between a string of banks on a daily basis. The only brief respite came with a flight to Copenhagen for a tryst with Sheila Buckley. She had asked him to take her back with him but he had said it was too soon and would arouse suspicion. He travelled back from Denmark via Lebanon to Melbourne.

By now, the net seemed to be closing. Stonehouse had also attracted the attention of Australian immigration officials acting on information from overseas, and was under surveillance. Yet he might still have bluffed his way out had it not been for an unfortunate twist of fate. That autumn, police across Australia had been briefed to look out for Lord Lucan. When Victoria State Police asked Scotland Yard for more pictures of Lucan, they were also sent some of the missing MP – and he bore a remarkable resemblance to Joseph Markham!

Stonehouse was arrested when police pounced on his luxury flat at the seaside resort of St Kilda on Christmas Eve 1974. He at first laughed off the questions about his false identity but a love note from Sheila Buckley found in his jacket ended the pretence. It read: 'Dear Dum Dums [her pet nickname for her lover]. Do miss you. So lonely. Shall wait forever for you.'

Buckley flew to Australia to be at his side. So too did Stonehouse's 45-year-old wife Barbara who, after twenty-four years of marriage, was initially elated that her husband had been found alive. Her joy was brief and, learning of the existence of 'the other woman', she quickly returned to the UK to file divorce papers. The fugitive's mistress remained in Australia until June 1975 when he was extradited back to Britain.

Stonehouse was held on remand in London's Brixton Prison, holding on to his parliamentary titles until August when he finally agreed to resign as MP and privy counsellor. By then, and by the strangest quirk of politics, Stonehouse held the balance of power in Britain. The reason was that his resignation put the Labour government, then headed by James Callaghan, in a minority with 315 seats compared to the 316 held by opposition parties. The subsequent by-election for Stonehouse's Midlands constituency was won by a rival Conservative candidate.

In court, Stonehouse conducted his own defence to twenty-one charges of fraud, theft, forgery, conspiracy to defraud, causing a false police investigation and wasting police time. On 6 August 1976, after a sixty-eight-day trial, he was found guilty on eighteen counts of theft, forgery and fraud and given a seven-year sentence. Sheila Buckley received a suspended two-year sentence for aiding and abetting him.

The trial judge's description of Stonehouse as 'an extremely persuasive, deceitful and ambitious man' failed to deter Sheila Buckley. She waited for him for three years – through three heart attacks suffered in prison and consequent open-heart surgery – to take back a bankrupt and seriously ill man. After his early release in 1979, he worked as a volunteer fundraiser for a London-based social action charity, Community Links. He joined the Social Democratic Party, which later merged to become the Liberal Democrats.

Buckley and Stonehouse married in secret in 1981 and, for the next few years, the MP tried his hand at thriller writing but he failed to make it big as an author. Perhaps his imagination couldn't compete with the astonishing exploits of the real John Stonehouse. On 14 April 1988, at the age of 62, he died of a massive heart attack. Sheila said of him: 'I've never met a man like him. John was gentle with everybody and, in particular, with me. I'll miss him forever.'

In December 2005, previously unseen documents released from the National Archives under the thirty-year rule revealed how British diplomats working for Harold Wilson's government obtained a confidential psychiatric report on Stonehouse as he fought extradition. It concluded: 'Stresses in his career led to a degree of disillusionment with himself. Mr Stonehouse suffered significant but "atypical depression". He thought of suicide but, deciding this was not the answer, devised a "suicide equivalent" – his disappearance from a beach in Miami.'

Stonehouse himself had previously come up with his own explanation for his vanishing trick:

> My wish was to be released from the incredible pressures being put on me, particularly in my business activities and various attempts at blackmail. I considered, clearly wrongly, that the best action I could take was to create a new identity and attempt to live a new life away from these pressures. I suppose this can be summed up as brainstorm or a mental breakdown.

None of which explained the final twist in the tale of the flamboyant fugitive. For in 2010, previously classified papers were released supporting suspicions that Stonehouse had worked as a Czech spy during the 1960s. The MI5 documents revealed that the then Prime Minister Margaret Thatcher had agreed in 1980 to cover up the revelations because there was insufficient evidence to bring him to court for a second sensational trial.

Art Forgers
Masters of the Trickster's Trade

'You can sell anything to Americans and Englishmen,' said the grandson of French painter Jean François Millet when convicted of forgery in 1935. 'They know nothing about art. Even their experts know nothing. All you have to do is to ask a fabulous price.' Many forgers before and since would agree with Millet's verdict on the gullibility of the leading lights of the art world. The forgers' only argument with Millet might be that the trade in fakes is not confined 'to Americans and Englishmen' – although most of the victims catalogued below are. Nor is it peculiar to modern times, for fakes have been with us for as long as a talented rogue has picked up a paintbrush or chisel.

History's best known artist, Michelangelo di Lodovico Buonarroti Simoni, not only created masterpieces such as the marble sculpture of *David* and the painting in the Sistine Chapel, he also dabbled in fakery. He first came to fame when he sold a marble *Cupid* to Cardinal San Giorgio, who then summoned him to Rome in 1496. It produced much needed funds for the struggling young artist. What he never told the cardinal was that he had stained and buried the statue to 'age' it as an antique.

One of the most prolific sculptors of all time was Giovanni Bastianini – and every one of his works was a fake. The nineteenth-century Florentine forger turned out terracotta busts by the dozen for a crooked art dealer. Before his death in 1868, Bastianini was heartened to see them displayed in museums and galleries around the globe. According to London's Victoria and Albert Museum, which took two of the forgeries, the faker's works were 'perfect examples of Renaissance sculpture'.

In more recent times, museums and galleries throughout the world have been regularly fooled by fakery. It took modern technology, rather than masterful knowledge, to uncover a fake that had been displayed as one of the most prized possessions of America's Cleveland Museum of Art. The museum believed that its wooden *Madonna And Child* had been carved in Italy in the thirteenth century. In fact, the work was indeed that of an Italian – having been carved by art restorer Alceo Dossena in 1920. In 1927 *Madonna And Child* was X-rayed to deduce whether such an ancient work was due for restoration. The discovery of modern nails embedded in the wood prompted the statue's sudden removal to the museum basement. Within three weeks, the Cleveland museum authorities had found a suitable replacement for the fake. They purchased a marble statue of *Athena* for $120,000. Unfortunately, it too was the work of Alceo Dossena, master forger!

Another gallery which paid handsomely for a string of fakes was the renowned New York Metropolitan Museum of Art. One particular statue, a 2-metre tall figure of an Etruscan warrior, held pride of place. One arm was missing, as was the thumb of his other hand. This was not surprising, as it had supposedly been buried since pre-Roman times. The museum had paid $40,000 for the statue in 1918. It was not until 1960 that Alfredo Fioravanti announced that he and five accomplices had created it – and, to prove it, produced the warrior's missing thumb, which fitted perfectly.

The Metropolitan Museum was again in trouble in 1975 when one of its most popular attractions, a beautiful bronze horse supposedly of the Greek period, was shown to be a fake and had to be withdrawn. In 1984 the museum was forced to re-examine many of its masterworks and discovered that a further forty-five of its treasures were fakes.

One of the main reasons given by artists for embarking on the trade of fakery is their disdain for the ignorance of art 'experts'. Another reason is their disgust at gallery owners' greed. That was certainly the case with perhaps the cheekiest of all forgers: Tom Keating, a talented Briton who had cheating down to a fine art, literally. For two decades, he recreated on canvas the paintings of more than 100 famous artists. His output of about 2,500 fakes was an incredible feat, worthy of admiration in the eyes of anyone but the art world and, of course, the law. What was even more amazing was the fact none of the fashionable dealers who handled his prodigious output recognised these blatant forgeries. Moreover, Keating did not wish to reap huge financial reward for his handiwork; he simply wanted to shame the self-styled elite who run galleries and art shops.

Born into poverty, the Londoner went to art college but, to his bitter disappointment, failed to gain a diploma. His work, he was told somewhat ironically, 'lacked original composition'. This early setback made Keating bitter and cynical about the art world. He was frustrated further when he was forced to reject a rare offer from a gallery to exhibit his paintings because he couldn't afford to frame them. He also became enraged by the huge mark-ups made by greedy dealers, once proclaiming: 'They are just East End blokes in West End suits. They don't give a damn about the paintings. All they're after is profit.'

Keating made a modest living as a freelance picture restorer, thereby learning valuable skills which he put to dubious use in 1950 when he embarked on what he called his 'fake period', referring to his works of art as 'Sexton Blakes' – London Cockney rhyming slang for fakes. He became a master at imitating the styles of Rembrandt, Goya, Constable, Turner, Gainsborough and Renoir.

What he didn't sell through auction rooms he gave away. He said one went to a tramp and another to a harassed mother of six he bumped into in a Woolworths store. This cavalier attitude may explain why it took so long for Keating to be exposed. For the recipients of his gifts would probably have sold them to junk shops and it would often take years before the painting surfaced in more conventional art outlets.

All it would have taken to discover Keating's counterfeits would have been a closer inspection and possibly a standard X-ray test, because he would usually write in white lead paint the word 'fake', add a rude word, or even sign his own name on the canvas before painting over it. In his Impressionist pictures, he often included tiny portraits of the artist whose work he was forging. His paintings were also coated with gelatin, which meant that the paint would lift off if ever cleaning was attempted.

In 1963, Keating read a book on the nineteenth-century artist Samuel Palmer and became captivated by him. He scoured art galleries for examples of Palmer's work to copy. At London's Tate Gallery, he touched one 'and a strange sensation went through me like an electric shock.' He claimed the spirit of Palmer would thereafter guide his hand. 'I'd sit in my little sketching room waiting for it to happen,' he explained. 'I have never drawn a sheep from life but then Palmer's sheep would begin to appear on the paper. With Sam's permission, I sometimes signed them with his name [because] they were his not mine. It was his hand that guided the pen.'

Dealers were so delighted that a lucrative market for Samuel Palmer had been created that if they had any doubts about the authenticity of the work, they kept them to themselves. Keating himself was less cautious and, after allowing a newspaper journalist to watch some of his methods, she was able to piece together the evidence that led to his exposure. However, the reporter, Geraldine Norman, admitted: 'I learned more in two weeks interviewing Tom than in seven years as *The Times* saleroom correspondent.'

The game was up but Keating simply shrugged off his sudden notoriety. He even happily cooperated with Norman on *The Fake's Progress*, a tongue-in-cheek account of his career. And he willingly confessed:

> My aim was to get back at unscrupulous galleries and dealers. Five or six times, dealers approached me to do copies and I did them. I was conned. Once a gentleman offered £65 to do two pictures after the style of [Dutch artist] Cornelius Krieghoff.

He gave me only £7.50 for them and hours later they were in a Bond Street gallery being offered at £1,500.

Tom Keating appeared in court at London's Old Bailey in 1977 charged with criminal deception. The trial was abandoned after five weeks due to his ill health but there had been some entertaining moments when he took the witness box. At one point, he was shown his most famous fake: an ink wash labelled *Sepham Barn 1831*, which had been sold as a genuine Samuel Palmer for £9,400. Keating turned to the jury and said: 'I am ashamed of this work.' He had no recollection of painting it and, contrary to his usual precision, he had used modern materials. The main figure of a shepherd was 'un-Palmerish' and the flock of sheep 'unsheep like'. It was the sort of painting, he said, that he would normally have burned or thrown away. Presented with another painting, a bemused Keating said: 'That must have taken me about half an hour. It's just a doodle. 'The 'doodle' had been bought at a country auction for £35. It was later sold by a London gallery for £2,550 – after 'expert' restoration work by the National Gallery.

To Keating's delight, the discomfiture of the art establishment, so ridiculed and acutely embarrassed in court, was immense. Moreover, his notoriety had won Keating what he had always craved as an artist: recognition. His works became highly prized. He was offered a £250,000 contract from one London gallery and a £30,000 commission for a single portrait. He turned both down. 'I have enough work to make me rich beyond my wildest dreams,' he said, 'but I have met many millionaires and they have all been miserable. All I have ever wanted is to paint. Painting is God's gift, not mine, and it should be used to bring pleasure.'

In 1983, Keating had the satisfaction of seeing Christie's auction house sell 150 of his paintings for almost £100,000. By the time of the following year's sale, the prices of his work had doubled but, sadly, he was not there to receive the plaudits. Tom Keating died in February 1984, aged 66. The stress of the court case had taken its toll but contributing factors were his years of chain smoking and the effects of breathing in the fumes of chemicals used in art restoring, including ammonia, turpentine and methyl alcohol. A newspaper described him as 'a charming old rogue whom the public warmed to.'

In 1992, a London collector bought what he believed to be a genuine 'fake' by Keating, only to find that it was a fake 'fake'. The artist who succeeded in exposing the sham of the art world could not have wished for a better accolade. After all, throughout his life, he had proved that imitation was the sincerest form of flattery.

Like Keating, David Stein was a gifted artist but felt that payments for his work were inadequate. Amazingly quick on the draw, Stein became the undisputed king of the art forgers for a brief four-year reign, during which he recreated the styles of some of the world's best-known artists, both living and dead.

The dead gave Stein no trouble but reproducing the living led to his downfall. On one occasion, while residing in New York in 1967, he rushed off three watercolours 'by Marc Chagall', which he had promised to a dealer. Working furiously in his apartment, the whole operation took just seven hours. During that time, he treated the paper with cold tea to give it the impression of ageing, meticulously emulated Chagall's style, forged the artist's signature and created phoney certificates of authentication. The delighted dealer was so proud of his acquisitions that he decided to show them off to a celebrated artist who had just arrived in New York ... Marc Chagall himself. Chagall's reaction was first bewilderment and then horror. 'They are not mine,' he said. 'And they are diabolical.'

Had Stein stuck to his regular fakes, recreating Cezannes, Renoirs or Manets, he would have got away with it. Instead he ended up in court accused of forgery and grand larceny. The case was not clear-cut, because embarrassed collectors refused to provide their paintings as evidence and New York art dealers refused to cooperate with the prosecution for fear of incriminating themselves.

'If only I had stuck to dead men,' he moaned as he was sentenced to three years in Sing Sing Prison. While in jail, he shared his knowledge of forgery with the New York Police Department, helping them create a special art forgery squad. On his release, Stein was deported back to his French homeland, where his previous misdemeanours caught up with him and he was back in jail for a further two and a half years.

His time in prison had given Stein the time to think about an honest, money-making venture and he hit upon the idea of painting famous people in the style of well-known artists. The gimmick made him a legitimate celebrity himself. For instance, from a single, thee-hour sitting he painted actress Brigitte Bardot in twenty-five different styles, ranging from Picasso to Van Gogh.

Up until his death in 1999 at the age of 64, David Stein remained bitter about the fickleness of art dealers and collectors. But he reckoned he had the last laugh. 'A lot of the art world is fake,' he said. 'They may not know it but there are about two or three hundred of my forgeries still on the market listed as originals.'

Most art forgers' talents are hidden, for obvious reasons. Eric Hebborn was different. The genial Englishman was among the most successful and prolific artists of his generation. An ex-Borstal boy who started his fakery as a penniless London art student, his drawings can still be found in great private collections and in galleries and museums around the world. Yet Hebborn could never be honoured for his services to art; instead, he was destined to become known as one of the greatest fakers of all time.

Hebborn copied almost every important European painter from the fourteenth to the twentieth century and created more than 1,000 'Old Master' drawings which have been attributed to the likes of Van Dyck, Gainsborough, Poussin and Degas. Yet he insisted that he was no conman because none of his drawings was a copy; each was a fresh work that recreated the style of a past great artist.

In later life, Hebborn was rumoured to have had links with the Mafia, which might explain his mysterious death. He was found bludgeoned to death in a Rome street in 1996 at the age of 62. He left a posthumous guide to fakery, *The Art Forgers Handbook*, in which he described his craft as 'a glorious game', a way of entertaining himself. He readily admitted his glee at deceiving the pundits. 'I have never tried to fool the man in the street,' he said. 'Only the "experts" are worth fooling, and the greater the expert the greater the satisfaction.'

Among the masters of artistic counterfeiting, a stateless Hungarian called Elmyr de Hory could claim to be the recipient of the greatest accolade of anyone in his line of business. He was the subject of a book titled *Fake*. It was written by fellow forger Clifford Irving, creator of the phoney 'Howard Hughes autobiography' catalogued elsewhere in this book.

De Hory was a fine artist in his own right. Born in 1911, the son of land-owning parents, he went first to an art school in Budapest, then the Akademie Heimann in Munich and finally to the Académie de la Grande Chaumière in Paris. His work gained him early recognition and his charm won him friends among famous artists such as Matisse and Picasso – although he would later have no qualms about imitating them for financial gain.

At the outbreak of the Second World War, de Hory was arrested in Hungary as a suspected spy then interred in a Nazi concentration camp for being both Jewish and homosexual. He survived but the end of the war saw him a broken and penniless refugee struggling to make a living in Paris. However, a chance remark by a visitor to his studio was to set him on the road to unforeseen profit. Spotting a line drawing by de Hory of a young girl's head, the visitor asked: 'Is that a Picasso?' De Hory did not demur. Instead he accepted the equivalent of £50 for the picture – then went on to paint another half a dozen 'Picassos'.

Ultimately, de Hory became so adept at recreating Picasso's work that the great man himself was once fooled. De Hory had the cheek to ask Picasso to authenticate one of his fake nude paintings. Readily putting his name to it, Picasso remarked: 'I remember painting her. It did take rather a long time to complete as I could not resist making love to her.'

After falling out with a partner in his crooked business, in 1947 de Hory fled Europe, ending up in Los Angeles, where the same attributes that had won him friends in Paris soon earned him a place among Hollywood's smart set. Calling himself Baron de Hory, he turned out paintings supposedly by Matisse and Renoir, which were snapped up by the rich residents of Beverly Hills. In 1952, after a sharp-eyed dealer spotted a fake, supposedly by Italian painter Amedeo Modigliani, de Hory swiftly moved to New York, where he knocked out fake Modigliani drawings at $1,000 a time.

The seasoned fraudster briefly tried and failed to live off his own work before falling back on forgery. He claimed he could paint a classic portrait in forty-five minutes, draw a 'Modigliani' in ten and then immediately knock off a 'Matisse'. During the late 1950s and early 1960s, de Hory was making about $250,000 a year from his fakes, allowing him to throw fabulous parties attended by glittering stars such as Marilyn Monroe. It is estimated that throughout his career his forgeries sold for more than $50 million in today's value.

De Hory finally settled on the Spanish island of Ibiza, where he bitterly complained: 'The art dealers, the experts and the critics resent my talent because they don't want it shown how easily they can be fooled. I have tarnished the infallible image they rely upon for their fortunes.' He was not to find peace on his Mediterranean hideaway, where he was in the clutches of a conman who controlled him and made a fortune out of his illicit work. The artist's tragic end came in 1976 when, after spending three months in jail on charges of homosexuality and consorting with known criminals, he walked free only to find dealers lining up to demand the return of their money. All this painted a future too grim for the ailing 70-year-old and, in a fit of depression, he killed himself.

In the recent history of infamous fakers, there is one who has been described as having committed 'the biggest fraud of the twentieth century'. John Myatt mimicked dozens of different artists, despite using techniques that were later derided as amateurish – one of his 'Monets' was created using Dulux house paints. Nevertheless, the end results were sold for hundreds of thousands of pounds to galleries and private collectors. Even after his court appearances in 1998, his authenticated 'genuine fakes' continued to sell for huge sums.

Myatt, a farmer's son, discovered his knack of mimicking other artists' styles while at art school in the 1960s, later putting this talent to use to subsidise his modest wages as a schoolteacher in Staffordshire. At first, there was no pretence that his output was anything but phoney. He advertised in the satirical magazine *Private Eye*: 'Genuine fakes. Nineteen and twentieth century paintings from £150.' One man who answered the advert, a charismatic character called John Drewe, saw greater potential and commissioned some 'Great Masters' to decorate his London home.

Among Myatt's output was a piece in the style of French Cubist Albert Gleizes, created one evening on his dining room table. Without the artist's knowledge, Drewe took the painting to Christie's, who valued it at £25,000.

Myatt said he could never forget the day Drewe telephoned him: 'He told me to sit down – then asked me how I'd like £12,500. I said I'd like it very much.' Unwittingly, that was the moment the honest, church-going lad from a farming background became one of the art world's most artful forgers. He admitted later: 'It didn't take me long to make the decision. It was the same amount of money as I could earn in a year as a supply teacher. I squared it with my conscience, saying no one was getting hurt.'

Pictures in the style of masters including Pablo Picasso, Henri Matisse, Roger Bissière, Marc Chagall, Jean Dubuffet, Alberto Giacometti, Ben Nicholson, Nicholas de Stael and Graham Sutherland followed. At the time of his arrest, police estimated Myatt had painted 200 forgeries to a regular schedule, delivering them to Drewe in London. The scam 'just grew' Myatt confessed. 'The problem was I didn't admit to myself it was criminal. It all seemed a bit unreal. John Drewe would just ask me to do paintings and I'd deliver them to him. He handled all the selling, passing them off as lost originals.'

Drewe created suitably fake histories for the paintings, which he sold for an average of £30,000. He used art gallery notepaper and forged receipts, and he even made fake entries in the indexes of major galleries such as the Tate and the Victoria and Albert Museum. Auction houses Christie's, Phillips and Sotheby's and dealers in London, Paris and New York were all the recipients of the forged works. Cheekily, Drewe donated £20,000 to the Tate, leading officials to trust him as a 'serious researcher'.

Meanwhile, Myatt was finding it increasingly hard to reconcile such dishonesty with his Christian faith. He confided his fears to Drewe, who agreed the scam would come to an end, but the parting of the ways was acrimonious.

In 1994, an anonymous tip-off brought police knocking on Myatt's door and the shamed artist immediately confessed. He offered to return £18,000 of his ill-gotten gains and to help convict his accomplice – although that process took four years because Drewe kept jumping bail. In September 1998 a penitent Myatt, then aged 53, stood in the dock at London's Southwark Crown Court as an astonished jury heard how the forgeries were produced. Some of the fakery was so blatant that lawyers were amazed how anyone could have been taken in. Paintings were found to have been created from ordinary household emulsion with brand names including Dulux. They were aged with vacuum cleaner dust and mud or sometimes with coffee watered down with 'personal lubricant' KY Jelly. The police, who had recovered only sixty of the forgeries, claimed the two men made at least £1million from the start of the scam in 1986 until they were arrested in 1994, a figure denied by the pair.

Judge Geoffrey Rivlin QC described the case as 'extraordinary.' He said Drewe had been the 'chief architect, organiser and driving force behind a massive fraud' and had demonstrated that he was a 'highly imaginative master forger of documents'. Drewe, whom one dealer called a 'mad genius', was found guilty of conspiracy to defraud, two counts of forgery and one of theft. Despite his protestations of innocence, claiming 'a cesspit of festering corruption' in the art world had made him a 'scapegoat' to conceal 'international arms deals known to the government', he was sentenced to six years and served two.

Myatt, said to be 'deeply ashamed' of what he had done, was sentenced to a year in jail for conspiracy, though he was released after only four months. While serving his time in Brixton Prison, he drew pictures of fellow inmates and warders, using pencils and papers sent to him by his arresting officer. When released, he was commissioned by the same officer to paint his family's portrait. Other commissions followed from members of the prosecution team who wanted fake originals to adorn their chambers. In the following years, collectors paid up to £45,000 for his paintings. As Myatt explained: 'I'm painting in the style of the great artists so ordinary people can own beautiful artwork without having to spend millions.'

While John Myatt appeared to have survived his criminal days relatively unscathed, there remained many victims of his and Drewe's fakery. More than 100 art collectors were duped and it was reckoned that at least 120 forgeries were still in circulation. Myatt commented: 'Even if I could identify them, I wouldn't. What good would it do? If people have paid a lot of money for something they think is an original, there is nothing to be gained by retrospectively disillusioning them.'

Han Van Meegeren
Hapless Forger was Hailed a Hero

The major art forgers who featured in the previous chapter claimed, as an excuse for their fakery, that they were revealing the art world's ignorance and avarice. True as that may be, none of those bold souls would have declared to be acting heroically. There is one of their craft, however, who stands alone as the uncrowned king of counterfeiters – a veritable genius who not only shamed the elite of the art world but ended up a national hero.

This master of mimicry was a Dutchman named Han van Meegeren. Hailed as the greatest art forger of the twentieth century, he was responsible for recreating some of the finest examples from the classic 'Golden Age' of Dutch Masters. And although they were actually painted a full three centuries later, when presented to a rapt audience they were lauded by experts, critics and political leaders, raising van Meegeren from humble beginnings to wealth and prestige.

The exposure of this brilliant imposter came about due to an unbelievable catalogue of events that followed the fall of Nazi Germany in 1945. It led to the faker saving himself from the gallows with one of the most far-fetched defences ever heard in a court of law – by persuading a judge and jury that he was not a traitor to his country but a wartime hero.

The court appearance at the close of his career was only the latest of the struggles he had faced throughout his life as an artist. Henricus Antonius van Meegeren ('Han' for short) was born in the Dutch city of Deventer in 1889 to a harshly strict schoolteacher father and a gentle, loving mother. It was from her that he inherited his artistic talents but, while she praised his childhood drawings and paintings, his father would tear them up scornfully. This cruel behaviour did not deter the budding artist, however. Referring to those childhood days, he once said: 'I invented a world where I was king and my subjects were lions.'

In his teens, van Meegeren took up a place at the Institute of Technology in Delft, where he was highly regarded and gained the institute's gold medal for best painting by a student. At 23, he married his pregnant girlfriend, Anna de Voogt, the Sumatran daughter of a Dutch government official serving in the East Indies. Perhaps his sudden responsibilities affected his work because he was bitterly disappointed when he failed his final exams.

Van Meegeren and Anna moved to Scheveningen, then a small seaside town, where, during a lull in his painting, van Meegeren produced his first fake, a copy of the watercolour for which he had won the gold medal. Anna refused to let him pass it off as the original and the couple argued fiercely. It was the first of their frequent rows, many brought on by van Meegeren's series of mistresses. The marriage fell apart and Anna left to live with her grandmother. So in 1917 the artist was alone again, struggling at his easel but not producing any acclaimed work. His paintings were described as being of high technical standard but lacking in richness and quality. One major exhibition in the Hague in 1922 received harsh reviews. The fiercest came from revered critic Dr Abraham Bredius, whom van Meegeren never forgave, for one thing he could not stand was ridicule.

For many unrewarding years, the increasingly disillusioned painter was forced to make a living by designing Christmas cards. He added to his income by some art restoration and selling portraits to tourists. Van Meegeren was now no longer an aspiring young genius but a broken, frustrated artist aged 43. It was at this particularly low point in his life that he decided to become a professional forger, choosing the great Dutch master Johannes Vermeer as the first artist to imitate. Van Meegeren could not help but smile as he realised the fun he could have at the expense of the critics and art experts he so despised.

His choice of Vermeer had been deliberate: the seventeenth-century Dutch painter was the one most admired by Dr Bredius. There was another reason: one of van Meegeren's close friends, Theo van Wijngaarden, had also been a victim of Dr Bredius's bullying. Van Wijngaarden sincerely believed that he had discovered a Frans Hals painting and had even had it authenticated by art experts, but the picture was dismissed out of hand by Bredius. This was not the end of van Wijngaarden's dealings with Bredius, however. Seeking revenge, van Wijngaarden painted a 'Rembrandt' and four months later was again standing before the self-important art expert. Dr Bredius examined the picture and pronounced it as genuine. Van Wijngaarden then gleefully took hold of the painting and slashed it top to bottom with a palette knife just to witness the look of horror on his adversary's face.

Van Meegeren, meanwhile, had moved from Holland to a villa in the south of France to set about his secret work with great determination, application and patience. It was important that the materials he chose fooled everyone. And so anxious was he to make his masterplan work that he spent four years hunting down the very same pigments that Vermeer himself would have used. This was by no means an easy task, for Vermeer obtained his characteristic blue colour from the powdered-down semi-precious stone lapis lazuli. Van Meegeren did the same, paying extraordinary attention to detail, even grinding the pigments by hand so that the particles would look irregular when examined under a microscope. After great trial and error, he found that mixing phenol resin and oil of lilacs with the paints gave them the correct viscosity and fast drying properties.

Providing the right canvas was also crucial. It had to look old. Van Meegeren simply bought old, genuine ones and either cleaned them or painted over the original pictures. Finally, with not a detail overlooked, he prepared special brushes which would reproduce the smooth texture of Vermeer's brush strokes. Even before he started on his first 'Vermeer', van Meegeren had the ageing of the work down to a fine art. The process was completed in a specially built oven with electric elements. Again much patience was needed to obtain the right temperature and time – 105 degrees centigrade for two hours – to bake the picture and harden the paint without causing any damage to the canvas. At last, everything was perfect. Was it the scent of the lilac oil... or the sweet smell of revenge?

It took van Meegeren seven months to complete the great religious work *Christ and the Disciples at Emmaus*, his first and most brilliant forgery. In keeping with Vermeer's style, it was a strong, simple composition. Christ and his disciples were seated at a table near a window through which light poured in upon the scene.

Van Meegeren had thought long and hard about the challenging subject, for only one genuine 'religious' Vermeer existed for comparison. The forger concentrated on every detail of the phoney work, collecting as many seventeenth-century items as he could find, including pots, plates and chairs, to ensure he was copying authentic articles for his picture.

Having spent so many years trying to recreate the great master's work, van Meegeren had become not only obsessed with Vermeer, but virtually possessed by him. 'It was the most thrilling, the most inspiring experience of my whole life,' he recalled later. 'I was positive that good old Vermeer would be satisfied with my job. He was keeping me company, you know. He was always with me during that whole period. I sensed his presence; he encouraged me. He liked what I was doing. Yes, he really did!' However, what Vermeer would have thought of van Meegeren using a passing Italian tramp as a model for Jesus in his religious work, one can only conjecture.

When *Christ and the Disciples at Emmaus* was finished, it underwent van Meegeren's intricate, perfected ageing process. After applying a coat of varnish, he then had to set about 'cracking' it. As with all his other forgery techniques, van Meegeren had painstakingly practised this one over many weeks. Previous tests had proved that a genuine but worthless seventeenth-century oil painting could be stripped down to the last layer of paint. The last thin layer had the authentic cracks and van Meegeren had found that, as he painted the new picture over an old one, these original cracks came through. For good measure, he used a cylinder around which he rolled the painting, and then he filled in all the cracks with black Indian ink to give the appearance of the accumulated dust of three centuries. The final touch was another coat of varnish, this time in a brownish colour. Only when he was certain the picture would stand up to detailed scientific examination was he ready to make the public aware of this great 'rediscovered' Vermeer.

Van Meegeren first paid a visit to a member of the Dutch Parliament and explained how a Vermeer had come into his possession. It belonged to a Dutch family now living in Italy, he said. The owners wished to remain anonymous for personal reasons and had asked him to make the necessary approaches to determine the painting's authenticity. Naturally, van Meegeren continued, an expert would have to be called. Perhaps the illustrious Dr Bredius might like to cast an eye over this mysterious work? And that is how the pompous art expert came to authenticate the painting as indeed a Vermeer and to issue a certificate of authenticity.

The discovery was big news in the art world and the prestigious Boijmans Museum in Rotterdam bought the picture for £58,000. When it went on show in 1937, one newspaper hailed it as 'the art find of the century'. Dr Bredius took all the glory for the discovery, boasting:

> It is a wonderful moment in the life of a lover of art when he finds himself suddenly confronted with a hitherto unknown painting by a great master, untouched on the original canvas and without any restoration, just as it left the painter's studio. We have here *a* – I am inclined to say *the* – masterpiece of Johannes Vermeer of Delft.

Van Meegeren, who had not made public his involvement, paid a visit to the museum on a day he knew Dr Bredius and fellow experts would be there. The forger took one look at the 'Vermeer' and pronounced it a fake. He was ignored. This was the reaction van Meegeren wanted. He now knew the money he had received for the painting was quite safe. And any intention he originally may have had about admitting the forgery and returning the money had disappeared. He would instead have further fun at the expense of the pompous elite of the art world.

With the same attention to detail, van Meegeren painted two works in the style of Vermeer's contemporary Pieter de Hooch before returning to the artist who had helped him wreak such satisfying revenge with five further Vermeer forgeries. They sold for fantastic prices. In total, van Meegeren received the equivalent of £25million for his works at today's prices, enabling him to lead a life of luxury. He bought several properties and adorned them with fine and original works of art. He employed artist's models who were more than willing to become artist's mistresses. But his easy money also allowed him to slide into a dependency on alcohol, drugs and prostitutes.

Van Meegeren had explained away his wealth with stories that he had won high sums on the state lottery no less than three times. But with the advent of the Second World War, and the German invasion of Holland, a more sinister suggestion for his riches began to surface. Could he perhaps be involved with the Nazi regime? In fact, van Meegeren had already sold one of his Vermeer forgeries, *Christ with The Woman Taken in Adultery*, to Nazi leader Reichsmarschall Hermann Goering, Commander in Chief of the Luftwaffe, for almost £200,000. After the Nazis' downfall in 1945, Goering's priceless art collection was uncovered at his Bavarian mansion. Most of it had been looted from churches, galleries and private collections but among the collection was, of course, *Christ with The Woman Taken in Adultery*. Investigating agents discovered it had been purchased from van Meegeren, who was arrested – not for the crime of forgery but for being a collaborator.

The accusation that he had sold a national treasure to the enemy presented the artist with a bitter dilemma. If found guilty of being a Nazi collaborator, he could face the death penalty. The alternative was to confess to his faked works of art and risk ruin. Initially he maintained that he had acquired the painting through a family friend before selling it on, with no notion that it would end up in Nazi hands. Eventually, however, he admitted the painting in Goering's possession was not only a fake but a fake painted by him.

At first, his astonished interrogators refused to believe him. Then a novel solution to the claim was devised. Van Meegeren was ordered to paint a copy of *Christ with The Woman Taken in Adultery*. He refused to do this, saying he didn't copy works; he created them. To prove his innocence as a collaborator but his guilt as a forger, van Meegeren would paint an entirely new 'Vermeer'. Thus *Young Christ in the Temple* came to be. Undertaken in the somewhat stressful conditions of custody, it was not one of van Meegeren's finer forgeries but it was convincing enough.

Upon its completion, the faker declared: 'I had been so belittled by the critics that I could no longer exhibit my work. I was systematically and maliciously damaged by the critics, who don't know the first thing about painting.' The experts, he added, were 'arrogant scum'.

A commission was set up to evaluate other paintings van Meegeren said he had forged: at least fourteen works that had all been declared genuine and sold at prices reflecting their 'authenticity'. His techniques had been so skilful that even ultraviolet and infrared photography revealed no clues. Further, chemical tests showed that the pigments, thanks to van Meegeren's fastidious care, were genuine – with one glaring exception. When he painted *Christ with The Woman Taken in Adultery*, he had used cobalt blue for Christ's robe. It was a basic error, for that particular pigment was not used until the nineteenth century.

This mistake might alone have failed to clear van Meegeren of treason but his further evidence did. His argument was that, far from collaborating with the Nazis, he had courageously forced Goering to strike a bargain. The reichsmarschall had been allowed to take possession of the fake Vermeer only if 200 works of art looted from Holland by the Germans were returned. Incredibly, because he was so anxious to get his hands on the Vermeer, Goering had agreed. Unconvinced, one of the investigating officers challenged: 'You may have saved 200 minor works, but in exchange Goering acquired one of only a handful of paintings by Vermeer.' The forger's rejoinder was fiery: 'Fools! You're like the rest of them. I sold no Vermeer to the Germans – only a van Meegeren, painted to look like a Vermeer. I have not collaborated with the Germans. I have duped them.'

The court hearing, in November 1947, lasted just one day. It cleared his name of the stigma of treason but exposed him as a master forger who had 'corrupted' the art world. He was found guilty of deception and forging signatures but, mercifully, was given the minimum possible sentence: one year in prison.

Han van Meegeren never served his time. Neither did he ever paint again. For before starting his sentence he suffered a heart attack and died six weeks later, on 30 December 1947. Shortly before his death, he explained why he had devoted his later years to reproducing the work of other artists in a bid to fool art experts and dealers. He said: 'I had to prove, once and for all, their utter incompetence, their shocking lack of knowledge and understanding.'

The ingenious fraudster would have enjoyed one of the many epitaphs that followed his demise: 'He epitomised that heroic figure, the victorious underdog; a little man, a forgotten failure and outcast who had accumulated by guile a vast fortune and fame at the precise expense of those who had refused him recognition.' His death had brought van Meegeren not only recognition as an acclaimed artist but as a hero of his homeland too. And that was not a bad legacy for a convicted forger.

Daniel Faries
Boss of the 'Jailhouse Shopping Co.'

Daniel Faries was a petty crook and, judging by the number of times he was caught, not even a very clever one. He spent most of his adult life in houses of correction, where not much seems to have been done to correct him. When he wasn't behind bars, he was leaning on them getting drunk. And when he wasn't drunk, he was drying out.

In March 1986 Faries was halfway through a course of treatment at a clinic in Jacksonville, Florida, when he decided to go back on the booze in a big way. A pal of his was having a party down south in the fleshpots of Miami, so Faries broke out of the clinic, stole a van and hightailed it to where the action was. It was some party. After two days' solid drinking, the shindig degenerated into arguments and brawls. Faries said later that someone handed him a gun and, although he couldn't recall why, he shot his old pal three times in the head. Surprisingly, he survived but when police raided the house and discovered the trappings of drug-taking, the injured man was questioned and taken to hospital. The following evening, police were again called to the house where they found Faries in the backyard, unconscious and reeking of booze, with the gun in the waistband of his trousers. He readily confessed to the shooting – and unfortunately, when his buddy died in hospital two months later, found himself charged with first-degree murder.

For the next four years Daniel Faries was locked up in Miami-Dade County Prison awaiting trial. These turned out to be the most lucrative years of his life as the failed small-time crook proved himself to be an inspirational entrepreneur, running a multi-million-dollar business from within the prison. His cell had cheap furniture, curtainless windows and bare walls but it became his 'executive office' where, under the eyes of the guards, he made a fortune from fraud.

Faries shared a dormitory-style cell with up to thirty inmates and, because they were all on remand, they had access to a telephone in the cell. As it says in the Florida Administrative Code, section 33-8.009 (9): 'Each inmate shall be provided with reasonable access to a telephone at reasonable times... .' The battered black telephone provided by Florida's prison service was the key to Faries's nefarious trade. It was all he needed to let his fingers do the stealing – the only tool he needed to pull off one of the most fantastic, yet little known, frauds in history.

While awaiting trial, Faries's phone was seldom silent as he skilfully used it to defraud credit card owners. With other people's card details, he ordered goods and services for accomplices on the outside, for his fellow jailbirds, for himself, even for his prison guards. His business, which became known among Miami villains as the 'Jailhouse Shopping Network', boomed to the tune of $3million. This is how it worked...

First Faries would phone his pals and tell them to go 'dumpster diving': slang for rummaging around in skips and rubbish bins looking for discarded credit card slips. Faries knew how careless people could be with their carbon receipts that contained the name and number of the cardholder. Armed with the numbers from his 'divers', Faries would then phone the credit card companies pretending to be a retailer checking on a sale. Thinking it was a genuine enquiry, they would give him the address and the credit limit of the cardholder.

The fraudster would then call, say, an electrical store and order their most expensive hi-fi, paying over the phone with the credit card details he had just been given. In case the firm checked, he would ask that the hi-fi be delivered to the cardholder's real address at a particular time. Faries would then call his 'diver' with details of the purchase, the time it was to be delivered and the name and address of the cardholder. At the appointed hour, the 'diver' would hang around outside the address. When the delivery van drew up, he would saunter over and say: 'Hey. I'm Mr So-and-so. That's my new hi-fi you've got there. Thanks a lot.' He would sign for the package, wait till the van had driven off, then head straight for the city where any one of a thousand 'fences' would give him hard cash for the goods.

The downside was that thousands of shocked credit card holders would look at their statements every month and discover they had bought a new TV, a slap-up meal at a top restaurant, an airline ticket to South America or a new Armani suit, courtesy of Faries and his amazing jailhouse shopping fraud. But the scam worked like a dream and, from his 'office' in cell 10 B 3 of Miami-Dade County Prison, Faries was becoming on paper a very rich man.

Sometimes, if he wasn't sure of an address, he would have goods delivered to the jail itself. The stores and card companies never checked – although the delivery drivers and prison guards must have raised an eyebrow at the high-class merchandise passing through the prison gates. Faries and his fellow inmates soon became the best-dressed convicts in America, wearing designer jogging suits and flash jewellery. 'Oh, yes sir, I had a bumper business,' Faries told a jail visitor later. 'It's so easy to find confederates. I never took more than half. I split half with everybody. I got robbed a lot but you just take it on the chin. Heck, it's all free.'

Even when credit card companies began to abandon the idea of carbon receipts, Faries had an answer. He formed a network of crooked sales assistants at shops, bars and restaurants and paid them $20 a piece for every card number they gave him. He would get his team to ask the cardholders to jot down their addresses and phone numbers so they could 'check the card's authenticity'. Grateful cardholders were happy to oblige, impressed at such security measures which prevented their precious cards falling into the wrong hands. Little did they know that the information they were providing would be relayed by phone to a cell block.

Faries was beginning to look upon himself as a Robin Hood character. He reasoned that the smart cardholder, after the initial shock of seeing their outrageous statement at the end of the month, would promptly contact the authorities and have the offending item struck from the bill. It would be the profit-bloated card companies who would ultimately pick up the tab. Faries's Jailhouse Shopping Network even branched out into the world of philanthropy. He used the stolen credit card numbers to pledge thousands of dollars to charity – starving children, the homeless, the sick and the aged. All from the phone in cell 10 B 3.

The extravagant conman also ordered presents for his cellmates and their relatives. If a fellow inmate was unable to celebrate his wedding anniversary because he was locked up, Faries would make sure that his wife got a bunch of roses and a gift of jewellery, bought with some unsuspecting victim's credit card. Faries subsequently claimed that his guards also got their fair share of his ill-gotten largesse. 'All the correctional officers knew what I was doing,' he told a reporter when the story of his prison business reached the Florida newspapers. 'Their families knew what I was doing because they were receiving gifts on every holiday, birthday and anniversary.' Faries told a CBS television newsman: 'The officers are just working stiffs, they're not making much money, and they're seeing all this stuff going on. They're hearing about Dom Perignon champagne and trips to the Caribbean. So I try to send things at Christmas and on holidays.' The interviewer then asked Faries what it cost the guards. He replied: 'Oh no! Perish the thought. No sir!'

Prison officials naturally denied accusations about gifts from Faries but there was no secret made of his generosity towards charities. Faries's explanation was that, with nothing to do in his cell but watch television, he would see reports of famine and hunger and would immediately get on the phone to pledge a credit card donation. He reckoned that if the victims of his frauds had actually seen the television pictures of famine victims, they'd have made the donation themselves anyway.

The first major snag in this otherwise smooth operation came in September 1987 when Faries, ever generous with other people's money, decided to hold a party for a group of inmates who were all being released at the same time.

Using the credit card number of an unsuspecting Dr Felix Entwhistle, he booked a suite at the luxurious Mayfair House Hotel in downtown Miami. From his cell, the unselfish Faries ordered the best champagne and classiest call girls for his newly freed chums. And throughout the night, they toasted the unwitting benefactor whose gold card was making the evening possible.

By midnight, however, a member of the hotel staff, concerned at the quality of the guests who hardly looked like a convention of eminent physicians, decided to check on Dr Entwhistle's credit limit. It amounted to $2,500, which by then had been well and truly spent. The hotel employee found a sober member of the raucous party and suggested that credit had run out. A call was made and within minutes an indignant 'Dr Entwhistle' was on the phone to the hotel's night manager, furious at the treatment of his guests. The credit limit was immediately extended, with an apology for spoiling the doctor's party.

Some weeks later, the real Dr Entwhistle was equally indignant when he got on the phone to his credit card company. Following his complaint, Detective Raul Ubieta of the Metro-Dade Police visited the Mayfair House Hotel to discover that no one, genuinely, could remember who had signed the bill as the party wound up. There was, however, a hotel record of a phone call made from the suite that night. It was a local number: 5454494. Detective Ubieta dialled it and got through to prison cell 10 B 3.

The game appeared to be up for Faries. A special Metro-Dade Police investigation unit, headed by Ubieta and fellow officer Lieutenant Ross, moved in on the Jailhouse Shopping Network. They bugged the phone in Faries's cell and recorded all numbers dialled. Ubieta was stunned by the result. 'We'd never seen anything like this,' he said. 'He was making orders all over the place for everybody – airline tickets, video equipment, computers, clothes. The hours he worked were outrageous.' Sometimes police noticed a sharp decrease in the number of calls and they were worried that Faries might have smelled a rat. But an informant would tell them that the 'managing director' of the Jailhouse Shopping Network was high on drugs. Faries had simply taken a day off.

To curb the flow of misappropriated goods, Ubieta and his team would try to intercept the items that Faries had ordered over the phone. 'I'd call the suppliers and point out to them they had just been the victims of a fraud,' said Ubieta. 'Many of them got angry and said that the card was genuine and that they had checked the address and phone number. They were furious that they were losing trade. I never mentioned to them that the number belonged to a prison. They would never have believed me.'

The police evidence against Faries was building up nicely when, within weeks, their case collapsed around their ears. Miami-Dade Corrections and Rehabilitation Department, who understandably had not been informed of the police investigation since some of their officers were on uncomfortably close terms with Faries, organised a search of cell 10 B 3. They found 300 stolen credit card numbers, with names, addresses, phone numbers and credit limits, requests for merchandise and even the scribbled text of messages to go with flowers ordered over the phone. Police were furious at the cell shakedown. They had hoped to gain enough evidence to nail not only Faries but also his associates working on the outside and, hopefully, any prison officers who might be on the take. Instead, they had to cut their losses, believing that at least they had enough evidence to get a conviction against the mastermind himself. When they confronted him following the cell raid 'he was no problem', recalled one of the officers. 'He showed us how he did everything. He told us he'd order up lobster dinners from the guards and how they allowed him to get laid during visits.'

Metro-Dade Police handed over all their statements and evidence to the Florida State Attorney's office and waited for fraud charges to be brought against Faries. But nothing happened. At first, they were told that charges would have to wait, pending the outcome of Faries's murder trial. Then, months later, the case against the Jailhouse Shopping Network was suddenly dropped. No official reason was given, although a state attorney's office official was reported as saying: 'There is very little deterrent value in bringing a couple of minor felonies to court when a guy is facing the electric chair.' In 1989, to the annoyance of the police, the state attorney's office closed the case once and for all. It said that using the evidence of an accused murderer against prison guards could not lead to a successful prosecution.

Meanwhile, Faries had been moved from cell 10 B 3 to cell 104 in the nearby Interim Central Detention Center – incredibly, still with access to a phone. On hearing this, shocked police investigators demanded a meeting with the Department of Corrections, only to be told that there was 'no legal basis for imposing prohibitions or restrictions on inmates' access to a telephone.' The fraudster was still in business. In fact, he was delighted with his new office. He had cell 104 to himself and shared the phone with only five other inmates in other cells. He said later: 'About the only difference the move made was to give me some more privacy. I didn't have so many people looking over my shoulder all the time.'

The only problem faced by the 'managing director' was that his stock of credit card numbers had dried up, having been confiscated from his cell by prison authorities. So, as he later revealed (in a 1991 interview for the TV show *Sixty Minutes*) he came up with a new corporate strategy. 'After the raid I still had one hidden card number, written on the bottom of my bunk. It was a woman's card. Regina Donovan was the name. It was a good number and I said, "Well here we go – we gotta do something!"' Faries took out an advertisement in the national newspaper *USA Today*, calling himself Regina Donovan Cosmetics. It advertised $90 of top-quality women's cosmetics for the bargain price of

$19.95, all credit cards accepted. Faries hired an answering service in New York for a week and the calls flooded in. There were no cosmetics, of course, but the callers dutifully left their names, addresses, card numbers, expiry dates... all the information that Faries needed. As he explained:

> The girls took the orders, saying 'Thank you for calling Regina Donovan, may we help you and what credit card will we be using today?' They wrote down the number and the expiry date, and at the end of the day I'd call them and they'd have this whole new stack of numbers. It was like a goldmine.

Business boomed and, in a fit of generosity, Faries even ordered an expensive set of weights and work-out equipment for the detention centre gym.

By early 1989 Faries had managed to postpone his murder trial date several times simply by firing one defence lawyer after another. Around this time, however, a telephone company called TELCO noticed that the number of long-distance calls made on fraudulent credit card numbers had increased in Southern Florida by a staggering 4,000 per cent. Painstakingly, the company went through the figures and were surprised to discover that no fewer than 1,500 of these calls could be traced to the telephone outside cell 104 of the Interim Central Detention Center in Dade County. TELCO bypassed both the police and the Corrections Department and called in the US Secret Service. The Jailhouse Shopping Network was about to go into liquidation.

It took ten months for federal agents to get sufficient evidence against Faries. During that time they established documentary proof that he had stolen $750,000, although the truer figure was probably nearer $4million. They raided Faries's cell twice and found thousands of credit card numbers. One senior agent asked the Department of Corrections why, in the light of the previous police investigation, Faries was still allowed near a phone. He was told that there was an administrative rule that 'this particular class of prisoner in this particular cell block was entitled to access to a telephone.' Rules were made not to be broken.

Faries was locked in his cell twenty-four hours a day while the Secret Service prepared a case against him. During that time, he was allowed to use the phone for only fifteen minutes, and then under the strictest supervision. But, Faries later claimed, business went on as usual. He boasted that he managed to run a telephone wire into his cell from the nursing office next door. Someone smuggled him in a phone and he rigged the whole thing up to his cell light so that, instead of ringing, the light flashed and the guards were not alerted.

However, even Faries could postpone his murder trial no longer. On 16 May, four years after the crime, he was convicted of the first-degree murder of his partying pal and was sentenced to twenty-five years. Federal agents hauled him off to the Metropolitan Correctional Center in Chicago to await trial on fraud charges. Refusing a defence lawyer and choosing to represent himself in court, he pleaded guilty to one charge of fraud and was given a further five years' jail term. Faced with serving his time in a federal prison, Faries suddenly complained of paranoiac visions and went conveniently cuckoo. He was promptly dispatched to Charlotte Correctional Institution near peaceful Fort Myers, on Florida's west coast where, in the much higher-security state 'psychiatric facility', he claimed to have put the credit card business behind him. Cynics were not so sure.

Pete Collins was the man who knew more about Daniel Faries than perhaps anyone else. A teacher at Jackson High School who became fascinated by the fraudster's case, he met Faries and began collating material for a book on the amiable conman. In 1991 the row over lack of action taken to curb Faries's excesses became the subject of an investigation in the *Miami Herald,* principally due to the thorough research of Collins, by then a freelance writer based in Miami. He told a TV audience:

> When I was interviewing him you could call him up at any time
> of the day or night and he would be working around the clock.
> He was operating in as many as forty states. There were as many
> as 150 drop sites, dozens of employees, $750,000 documented in
> stolen goods – perhaps in reality up to two to four million dollars –
> and that was just during an eleven-month window of his captivity.

So how did Faries manage to operate his bizarre one-man crimewave for so long? Asked this question, the man in charge, Director of the Miami-Dade Corrections and Rehabilitation Department Lonnie Lawrence, commented: 'We don't have a perfect system.' But for Daniel Faries himself, the system was absolutely perfect. As he said:

> If they put you in a room the size of a bathroom for years at a time
> with only a telephone, you come up with some pretty inventive
> stuff, because everything you do, you do through the phone. I feel
> like I constructed a train, and just darn near anybody can drive a
> train. You don't have to be terribly intelligent and only marginally
> capable. Heck, it's on a track. All you have to do is put in the
> fuel – credit card numbers – and this train'll go! What I did was
> not really so smart. And there was certainly nothing very secret
> about it. It was all pretty wide open. On the outside of my cell
> door I had Mastercard and Visa logos.

Thérèse Humbert
Custodian of the Locked Chest

French peasant farmer Gilbert Aurignac neglected his fields to spend idle days in the cafes of the small town of Beauzelle, drinking himself into a stupor on cheap red wine. He would regale his fellow drinkers with unlikely tales of his family's former glory, of how his real name was the slightly grander d'Aurignac and how he had been disowned by his aristocratic father. But, he said, his two sons and two daughters would inherit vast wealth upon his death.

Aurignac's oldest child was Thérèse, born in 1860, and she too had heard her father's boastful story, so often that she believed it. When he died in 1874, however, she learned the truth: she, her sister and two brothers had been left paupers and she would have to take in washing to keep the family fed.

Thérèse Humbert had learned one simple truth in life: that the world is full of gullible people who will believe anything if it is repeated often enough. And although she was no beauty – the provincial washerwoman was as podgy as she was penniless – she had a certain magnetism that would win over the rich and famous. Her charismatic attraction would also win her the hand in marriage of a trusting husband and ultimately make her a fortune.

Thérèse took her first humble steps on her path to riches when she moved to the nearby city of Toulouse, where she went to work as a laundry maid at the home of the mayor, an ambitious lawyer and politician named Gustave Humbert. There she began to employ the inventive talents that she had learned from her father – but to much greater effect. First, she allowed herself to be seduced by her boss's son, Frederic, to whom she wove the most astonishing story. As a youngster, she said, she had attracted the attention of a rich spinster named Mademoiselle de Marcotte. Now very old and without any surviving relatives, this venerable lady had written a will bequeathing to Thérèse her entire estate, including its chateau and vineyards.

Frederic believed every word of her tale, fell madly in love with her and, despite the protestations of his father, secretly married her. He took her to Paris, where he launched a career as an advocate. The fees he earned, however, were wholly insufficient to sustain the extraordinary spending of his ex-washerwoman wife. She fell in love with 'Gay Paree' and entered into the social whirl. On the back of her 'inheritance' the couple borrowed more and more money – until one day their creditors checked on the identity of her benefactor and found there was no such person as Mademoiselle de Marcotte.

Now, there were several things that Thérèse could have done. She could have fled the city. She could have stuck to her story. She could have owned up to her fraud. Or she could simply pile fresh lies upon the old ones. Thérèse chose the latter course. Her story about Mademoiselle de Marcotte had indeed been untrue, she said, but she had fabricated the tale only to disguise the true identity of her benefactor. He was Robert Henry Crawford, a millionaire American from Chicago, whom she had met on a train two years previously. They had become friends and, when he subsequently suffered a heart attack, she had nursed him back to health. Mr Crawford had since died, however, and had left his fortune to be shared between his two nephews in the United States and Thérèse's younger sister Marie. Marie, then still a schoolgirl, would not receive her inheritance until she was 21 – but on reaching that age, Therese herself, as guardian, would receive from the inheritance an annual income of almost $100,000.

One of the people to whom Thérèse told this fresh pack of lies was her father-in-law, Gustave Humbert. The Toulouse mayor had risen rapidly in the world of politics and was now minister of justice in the national government. Whether or not he believed Thérèse's tale, she nevertheless persuaded him to pay all her and Frederic's Parisian creditors to avoid a family scandal. In turn, she 'repaid' old Monsieur Humbert by publicly announcing that the documents containing details of the inheritance had been placed by American lawyers in a locked safe, the administration and secure keeping of which had been guaranteed by the Humbert family until her sister Marie came of age.

As Paris buzzed with the story of the 'Crawford Inheritance', Thérèse boldly turned up at the bank to which she had previously owed the most money. Warmly welcomed by the manager, she told him: 'Sadly, Monsieur, I am not permitted to open the safe and exercise the bonds and securities therein until Marie comes of age. Otherwise, I am in danger of forfeiting all claim upon the Crawford millions.'

Predictably, she then asked for a loan. It was readily given. Thérèse repeated the trick at banks throughout Paris and elsewhere. One Toulouse bank alone advanced her seven million francs. Much of the money was used to purchase a lavish mansion in the capital, in her bedroom of which she installed a safe supposedly containing the secrets of her and her little sister's fortune.

The door of this massive, fireproof, steel structure was opened only once, when she invited an overawed provincial notary to examine a number of bundles of paper and to itemise the wrappers that supposedly indicated their contents. Then the safe was locked and thick wax seals were applied to the doors and handles. The imposing safe was not to be opened again until Marie's twenty-first birthday.

Meanwhile, Thérèse and Frederic embarked on an unprecedented spending spree. Thérèse also invited Marie and their two brothers, Emile and Romain, to join her in an orgy of extravagance. The human cash dispenser became known in Paris society as 'La Grande Thérèse', as the ample-bosomed lady swept in and out of restaurants and fashion salons and opera boxes.

Only one mishap threatened their idyll. A Lyon banker named Delatte visited Thérèse at her Paris mansion to arrange the advance of a further loan secured on the inheritance. Idly, he inquired of her where in America her late benefactor had lived. Off the top of her head, Thérèse replied: 'Somerville, a suburb of Boston.' Unbeknown to Thérèse, the Lyon banker was about to sail to the United States and, while in Boston, made enquiries about the fictitious millionaire James Henry Crawford. Discovering that no one had ever heard of such a person, Monsieur Delatte wrote to a fellow banker in France telling him of his suspicions.

Before further investigations could be made in the United States, however, Delatte mysteriously vanished. After a few days, his body was fished out of the East River, New York. He had been murdered. The killer was never uncovered but it has always been assumed that Delatte's untimely death was what would now be known as a 'contract killing', ordered by Thérèse or her brothers. And it took only the glib tongue of 'La Grande Thérèse' to calm the fears of the French banker to whom Delatte had written. The threat of exposure evaporated, as did the money that the Humbert clan continued to borrow, which had now reached an estimated sixty-five million francs.

There was one event that Thérèse Humbert could not influence, however: Marie's twenty-first birthday. The day was looming like a time bomb ticking away inside the great safe. Thérèse countered with two plans. The first was to distract attention from the vital birthday by inventing a dispute between herself and the non-existent American nephews over where the securities should be stored. Her second ploy was for her brothers to establish a finance house in a rented building in fashionable Boulevard des Capucines and to seek investment business through a chain of salesmen. Early investors found their returns swift and satisfactorily high, and the money flowed in. None of it was invested, of course. Apart from the small sums paid out in high 'interest', the rest was put aside to reimburse some of the more pressing creditors who wanted their loans repaid the moment Marie came of age.

The whole corrupt edifice began to collapse when a Bank of France official, Jules Bizat, investigated the invested funds of the Humbert brothers' finance house and found that there were none. He went straight to the prime minister, Pierre Marie Waldeck-Rousseau. Fearing that official involvement would precipitate yet another governmental scandal (there had already been several at the close of the nineteenth century) the premier decided to leak the story to the Paris newspaper *Le Matin*. Thérèse had no alternative but to protest her innocence while fending off the demands of creditors.

Now began an extraordinary chain of events. The Humberts' lawyer, Maitre du Buit, believed so fervently in the truth of the Crawford Inheritance that he threatened to sue the newspaper for libel and offered to open the safe to clear her name. This was the very last thing that Thérèse wanted, of course, and she panicked. On 8 May 1902, two days before the safe was due to be opened by du Buit, Thérèse or one of her accomplices set fire to the upper floor of her home. Everything in her bedroom was gutted, apart from the safe, which proved itself totally fireproof.

Thérèse, now enmeshed in a web of her own lies, assembled her sister, her brothers and husband Frederic, and took a train to an unknown destination. Thus, she was nowhere to be found when, on the appointed day, lawyer du Buit led an anxious band of businessmen and bankers into Thérèse's bedroom. The wax seals were broken, the doors were unlocked and eager hands swung them back to reveal... a single house brick!

Many years earlier, upon the death of Thérèse's boastful father Gilbert Aurignac, his children had stood around as Madame Aurignac turned the key in an old oak chest which, he had long bragged, contained papers documenting the family's secret fortune. It too had contained nothing but a brick. Now Thérèse was repeating history, though for a much more august company.

The aftermath of the discovery in her bedroom safe in 1902 reverberated around the social and financial circles of France. Ten suicides were attributed to her fraudulent machinations, one of the victims being a leading banker. But of the lady herself, there was no sign. Thérèse and her family remained undetected for seven months until Spanish police traced them to a Madrid lodging house. They were extradited and, in February 1903, she, Frederic, Emile and Romain were sent for trial on no fewer than 257 charges of forgery and fraud. On 8 August they stood in the dock at the Palais de Justice while, outside the court, queues formed of thousands of spectators from all over France.

Special trains had even been laid on, such was the fascination for this 'trial of the century'. They were disappointed to see that the arch trickster, 'La Grande Thérèse', was by now just a plump, sallow old woman whose once-magnetic personality had seemingly deserted her. A foreign newsman disparagingly called her 'a typical French cook'. Thérèse and Frederic were each sentenced to five years in prison. Romain got three years and Emile two.

After the trial, the famous brick, along with the charred metal safe surrounding it, went on display in a Paris shop window where it became something of a tourist attraction. Thérèse herself was released after three and a half years because of her good conduct in jail. She hid herself away in the countryside, living in obscurity and relative poverty until 1917 when, overshadowed by the horrors of the First World War, she died, her passing unreported and her deeds largely forgotten.

Rosemary Aberdour
Spending Spree of a Fake 'Lady'

Rosemary Aberdour, the plump only child of a comfortably-off middle-class English family, always knew she was destined for greater things. A dreamer from childhood, she was forever boasting about the riches she would one day acquire. Such grandiose visions must have seemed remote to neighbours in the little English village where she lived with her parents. But not even Rosemary herself could have envisaged the wealth and lifestyle that she would soon attain.

Rosemary decided at an early age that she was good at handling other people's money. While living at home with her parents, a doctor and medical secretary in the village of Wickham Bishops, Essex, she had helped raise funds for her local parish church. But already she was dreaming and scheming of unlimited funds of her very own. Even she could not have imagined how much, or indeed just how it was going to come her way, but the opportunity arose when she arrived in London and found that there was as much money at her disposal as she could lay her stubby little fingers on.

That she got away with it was incredible. Yet an inner confidence, plus a winning smile, were to see her through three years of lies, fraud and fantasy as she lived the life of an aristocrat, becoming rich off the generosity of others. In one period of just three months, she went through nearly £1.5million. There were lavish parties, expensive cars, made-to-order jewellery, luxury homes, vintage champagne and all the other trappings of a millionaire lifestyle – as led by her, under the assumed title of 'Lady Rosemary Aberdour'.

The route to Rosemary's success as a fraudster was simple: she took a course in bookkeeping, a skill which was to come in exceptionally useful when she was in a position to make the books balance greatly in her favour. That opportunity came in November 1986 when she successfully applied for a £20,000-a-year job at London's National Hospital for Neurology and Neurosurgery in Queen Square. The hospital had a development fund, a charity launched to raise £10million to build a new wing, and Rosemary was now determined to use

106

a proportion of the donations on herself. After organising a charity ball at London's Guildhall, attended by the Princess of Wales, she realised that this was the glittering life she wanted to lead and earnestly set about achieving it.

In July 1987 Rosemary's months of devotion to duty paid off. She was promoted to the charity's deputy director. It was a position of great trust. Rosemary was to bank all the cheques that came into the National Hospital Development Foundation and look after the accounts. At first, she stole a mere £500 to take herself on holiday but, once she realised she had got away with the theft, there was no stopping her. It was easy. Hundreds of thousands of pounds passed through her hands and she simply took the cheques for herself and fiddled the books.

Her golden opportunity came when she was asked to become chairman of the Queen Square Ball, a separate fundraising committee. The contents of its bank account were perused only when the date of the annual ball came around; the rest of the year it came under no scrutiny. Rosemary had all the time in the world to deposit money stolen from the National Hospital Development Foundation into the Queen Square Ball account and to use the account as her very own nest egg. She regularly stole cheques received in the post of between £20,000 and £100,000. Not content with having one source of illicit income, Rosemary started forging the signature of the charity's director Richard Stevens. She now had fraudulent cheques to increase her spending power. At last, money was no object.

When Rosemary wanted a new car, she bought one: a £70,000 Bentley. And, as always, she had an answer when asked about her purchase, made on the Queen Square Ball account, telling top-notch car dealers H. R. Owen that the millionaire's motor model was to be a raffle prize at the ball. Then there was the £171,000 of charity cash which Rosemary spent at top jewellers Boodle & Dunthorne, and her luxury new home in Kensington. She even sent her chauffeur to Harrods to buy fillet steak for her dog Jeeves.

It was incredible that no one ever delved into Rosemary's spending. But if they did, she had an answer for that too. 'I'm an heiress,' she would reply coyly. 'I have an inheritance of £20million.' No one disbelieved her. Hospital charity chairman John Young said Rosemary had a royal air about her and a 'great presence'. The fake Lady Aberdour would even arrive for work in her chauffeur-driven Bentley, regally waving at Mr Young.

There was no end to her cheek. She wrote to Richard Stevens enclosing a cheque for £100,000 which, she said, was her gift towards a new hospital ward and adding that her trust fund had given her permission to make donations totalling £500,000 towards this worthy cause over five years. Rosemary asked that her donation be received 'anonymously'. This was hardly surprising when she had stolen the money from a charity headed by Mr Stevens himself.

Rosemary loved the high life. There was no limit to her spending. She would go on wild sprees with her credit cards and think nothing of frittering away £30,000 on a weekend shopping jaunt. She also acquired a new circle of friends, people she felt would not question her aristocratic status too closely. She became renowned for her extravagant parties. As a supposed member of the aristocracy, a respected socialite and now a generous benefactor, she entertained lavishly. One party at her London home had a Caribbean theme. She employed professional party organisers to make sure every attention to detail was paid. Guests, wearing grass skirts and Caribbean shirts, arrived to find live lobsters in tanks of water, bars with Caribbean roofs made out of specially imported materials, two tons of sand, palm trees and champagne spouting from showers. It had taken seven days to 'build' the party, at a cost of £40,000. As one partygoer said: 'It was Rosemary living a dream. It was her going to the Caribbean for the weekend.'

Rosemary was never to explain why she decided upon 'Lady Aberdour' as her aristocratic pseudonym. But there was one particular family who felt she had a lot of explaining to do – the genuinely titled Aberdours. They only became aware of an impostor when a Sunday newspaper wrote about Rosemary. The writer thought it too audacious to question her face to face about her illustrious roots, so he looked the family up in the aristocrats' directory *Debrett's*, found the Aberdours and added Rosemary to their lineage!

It was now taking all Rosemary's nerve, not only to maintain her fake existence, but to avoid discovery over rapidly dwindling charity funds at the hospital. A scheduled visit from auditors meant Rosemary had to put in overtime to balance the books. She had to adjust figures, produce forged documents and transfer cash. She even raised an overdraft on the Queen Square Ball account. The auditors did not notice anything amiss. 'It was all done with stunning skill,' said John Young, who was again to fall victim to Rosemary's quick-thinking. She forged his signature to get her hands on even more cash and, when a building society manager queried it, she told them that 'poor Mr Young' suffered from Parkinson's Disease which made his hands shake.

By now, Rosemary knew deep inside that all the money in the world could not buy love or friends. She had no real companions, just hangers-on, and even they were beginning to tire of the party merry-go-round. It was always the same crowd of people, the same old Rosemary determined to put on a party more outrageous than the last and desperate to be the centre of attention. It was a sad fact that guests at some of her parties now mainly comprised staff and the most casual of acquaintances. 'She left all her parties early,' said partygoer Hamish Mitchell. 'It was as if she wasn't having a good time.'

Ever blinkered to the harsher reality of life, poor little rich girl Rosemary decided to cheer herself up with the biggest party ever. In fact, it was a fortnight of parties. The venue for the two weeks of total self-indulgence was Thornton Watlass Hall, a magnificent country estate in Yorkshire. Every night, the guests sat down to a gourmet dinner. There was live entertainment by top cabaret artists, firework displays, vintage car races and, of course, the best champagne on tap.

Perhaps living such a complex lie began to take its toll on Rosemary or perhaps she at last realised that the good life would have to come to an end. Whatever her reasoning, she was determined to give up her 'career' with as much extravagance as she had pursued it. She rented a £123,000-a-year London penthouse with its own swimming pool, which was to be the venue for yet more of her flamboyant hospitality. Then she embarked upon the spending spree of a lifetime. There were two £40,000 parties – first a Star Trek Voyage of Discovery Party which Rosemary hosted, followed by a friend's birthday party which took the form of a medieval banquet at Conwy Castle in Wales. Guests were flown in by helicopter. Then there was the Teddy Bears' Picnic party which cost a massive £70,000 to stage at top London hotel Claridge's. Other personal indulgences included a £9,000 'RUA' personalised car number plate for her Mercedes sports car, £78,000 to hire a yacht, £34,000 worth of vintage champagne and £54,000 on her favourite flowers, white lilies. At the height of Rosemary's frenzied spending in December 1990, she was getting through £15,000 every day. In just three months, she spent £1,350,000. By April 1991, Rosemary had all but exhausted the charity donations. For the first time, she began to owe people money.

A few weeks later, Rosemary knew it was all over. Charity director Richard Stevens found a letter in one of her office drawers. It bore the forged signatures of both himself and John Young. The letter was to the Abbey National Building Society, asking them to transfer £250,000. 'It was a very good forgery,' admitted Mr Young. He confronted Rosemary who, cool to the last, told him she had 'cash flow' problems and that the matter would be sorted out that very afternoon. It never was. Rosemary boarded a plane for Brazil along with new boyfriend Michael Cubbin, to whom she had recently become engaged. An Army helicopter pilot who had met Rosemary in a pub near her parents' home, Captain Cubbin had been unaware of her crimes. When she confessed, he persuaded her to return to face the music.

Back in London, Rosemary spent six months on remand – during which she received a new title, Prisoner Aberdour, number TT184 – before facing court to plead guilty to seventeen charges, including five of theft and eleven of obtaining property by deception. She had stolen and spent over £2,700,000. Her barrister Graham Boal compared her crimes to a compulsive gambling spree, saying she had an uncontrollable desire to 'please people' by attempting 'to buy their affection and esteem.' He said: 'The so-called friends, who sponged off her ill-gotten gains, have evaporated like the bubbles in champagne. The cars and the jewels have gone back to their rightful owners. The pretty balloons have long since burst and the party's over.' It was argued that the phoney Lady had nothing to show for the spree and that the only real victims of the crime were insurance companies, who had largely repaid the stolen loot to the charity.

Rosemary was sentenced to four years in prison. Newspaper reports labelled her 'Snooty Big Spender', 'The Girl Who Tried to Buy Love' and 'Phony Aristocrat'. And the Essex girl returned to Essex to serve her time, at Bullwood Hall Prison. Meanwhile, the National Hospital for Neurology and Neurosurgery was left to sort out the monumental financial fraud she had perpetrated. Managers of the National Hospital Development Foundation and the Queen Square Ball fund refused to accept the mess had been of their making. They blamed building societies and banks for failing to act the moment suspicions had been aroused. Under threat of legal action, the building societies involved paid back £1.5million, the banks nearly £1million. The charity was determined to recoup as much of its loss as was humanely possibly, serving writs on those who had provided services or goods in return for stolen money and fraudulent cheques. As one party organiser said: 'It all got pretty nasty.' Rosemary's furniture and paintings went back to the shops that had sold them and the money was refunded. Other possessions fetched around £100,000 at a sale organised by London auction house Christie's.

Rosemary served two years of her sentence and was released in October 1993. The hospital's long-awaited new wing, with its eight wards, opened three months later. A year later, in a modest ceremony at Rosemary's local church, back home in Wickham Bishops, the loyal Michael Cubbin married his by-now penniless fiancée. All her so-called friends had deserted her. Promises of million-pound book and film deals about her life had long evaporated. The party really was over. At the age of 32, the former 'Lady' may not have been able to buy love, but from her bizarre double-life, she had found it.

Arthur Orton
Tubby Imposter Branded a Big Fat Liar

It was one of the most far-fetched frauds of all time: a poor, fat, ugly, broke, uneducated butcher from the Outback of Australia laid claim to be the long-lost heir to an aristocratic fortune – and came within a hair's breadth of succeeding. In the course of what was the longest-running legal action in history, this unlikely imposter, going by the name of Arthur Orton, tried to prove that his real identity was Sir Roger Tichborne, son of one of England's premier families. His claim was not only implausible but downright absurd, yet the scoundrel's bumbling bid almost bore fruit.

So just who were the players in this extraordinary saga that gripped Victorian Britain? The real Sir Roger Tichborne was born in 1830, the eldest son of Englishman James Tichborne and his French wife Henriette, a wealthy Roman Catholic couple who lived in Paris. They had four children, only two of whom survived: Roger and his younger brother Alfred. When James Tichborne's brother, the tenth baronet, died without leaving an heir, Roger suddenly leapt to next in line to take the title.

Roger, a feeble lad prone to asthma attacks, was idolised by his mother who spoiled him and gave in to his every whim. His father, irritated by Henriette's obsessive love for their son, was anxious the boy should be whipped into shape, so sent him to a strict English boarding school, the Jesuit college Stonyhurst, in Lancashire. Four years later his father secured a commission for Roger in the Sixth Dragoon Guards, where he was nicknamed 'Small Cock', for reasons that will become clear.

In his early twenties, he fell in love with his cousin, Katherine Doughty, but their romance was doomed. The Roman Catholic Church did not allow first cousins to marry, and Katherine's family did not consider Roger a suitable match. Her father, Sir Edward Doughty, forbade the two to meet for three years. He told them that if they obeyed his instructions and their feelings were still strong for each other when the three years had passed, he would reconsider. He would even try to obtain dispensation from the Catholic Church to allow them to marry.

Roger and Katherine reluctantly agreed to comply with her father's wishes. They bade a tearful farewell, never realising it was the last time they would ever see each other. When Katherine had gone, Roger sat down and wrote a moving letter to her. It read:

> I make on this day a promise, if I marry my cousin Katherine Doughty this year, or before three years are over at the latest, to build a church or chapel at Tichborne to the Holy Virgin in thanksgiving for the protection which she has thrown over us, and praying God that our wishes may be fulfilled.

To prove his intent, Roger made a copy of the letter and gave it for safekeeping to a trusted friend, Vincent Gosport. He then resigned his commission and boarded a boat bound for South America.

Roger spent ten months trying to forget Katherine, scraping a living in Chile and Argentina. He then decided to head for the United States, and in 1854 the 24-year-old joined a small British trader, the *Bella*, leaving Rio de Janeiro for New York. He was never to complete the journey. The *Bella* went down in fierce Atlantic storms, the only trace ever found of her being the ship's logbook. There were no listed survivors. Roger's mother was overcome with grief at hearing the news. She blamed her husband for sending their beloved son away. Never recovering from the loss, James Tichborne died soon afterwards. Three years later, Roger Tichborne was officially declared dead, and the family estate and title were passed to Roger's young brother, Alfred.

Henriette felt the whole family was cursed. She had lost three of her children and her husband. But in her tortured mind, she believed that somehow her darling boy Roger would one day return and she began an international hunt for him. She placed advertisements in newspapers everywhere from South America to Australia seeking news of her son. On 5 August 1865, a front-page advert appeared in the Sydney newspaper *The Australasian*: 'A handsome reward will be given to any person who can furnish such information as will discover the fate of Roger Charles Tichborne ... the son of Sir James Tichborne (now deceased) and heir to all his estates.'

A copy of the newspaper fell into the hands of Arthur Orton, a semi-literate butcher from Wagga Wagga, in the Australian Outback. Under the assumed name of Thomas Castro, this ne'er-do-well had emigrated from the East End of London to escape his creditors and had settled in Australia with a wife and two young children. Orton's poor literacy prevented him fully understanding the meaning of the advert, but when it was explained to him, he decided to target the Tichborne family with a dastardly deception – seeking not only someone else's fortune but a baronetcy too.

Clutching the advertisement, Orton made his way to the office of a local lawyer, William Gibbes, and told him the incredible story that, although he was living under the name of Thomas Castro, he was in fact, the missing Roger Charles Tichborne. As proof, he showed the lawyer a pipe carved with the initials R.C.T. Gibbes was taken in by his story and wrote to Henriette in Paris, telling her that her son might indeed still be alive.

Henriette was overjoyed, replying immediately. She begged to learn more, asking that 'Roger' write to her himself. With some difficulty, in January 1866 Orton penned a letter addressed to 'My dear Mother' which went on:

> The delay which has taken place since my last Letter, Dated 22nd April, 1854, Makes it very difficult to commence this letter. I deeply regret the truble and anxiety I must have cause you by not writing before. Of one thing rest Assured that although I have been in A humble condition of Life I have never let any act disgrace you or my Family. I have been poor man and nothing worse.

The reply from the Dowager Lady Tichborne arrived in April. Her state of mind while writing it may well have been influenced by the fact that only three days earlier her youngest son Alfred had died of drink, leaving his baby son Henry as the twelfth baronet. She wrote: 'My dear and beloved Roger, I hope you will not refuse to come back to your poor afflicted mother. I have had the great misfortune to lose your poor dear father and lately I have lost my beloved son Alfred. I am now alone in this world of sorrow.'

A regular correspondence began between mother and 'son'. Henriette, in her desperation to believe her boy was still alive, apparently did not question the nature of Orton's letters, ignoring friends when they pointed out that the degree of literacy in them conflicted with the expensive education Roger had received at Stonyhurst. Henriette wrote to Orton to tell him to hasten to Sydney, where he would receive instructions for his passage to Europe.

Thus, with £20,000 borrowed on the strength of his new-found fortune, Orton arrived in Sydney and encountered the first hurdles between his outrageous claims and the Tichborne inheritance. In the city, he was interviewed by Francis Turville, private secretary to the Governor of New South Wales, who happened to be an old friend of the Tichborne family. Turville reported back that Orton was a strange character 'and dirty enough', yet was forced to admit that he made so little effort in convincing anyone he was an English aristocrat that he appeared 'the reverse of an imposter'.

Orton's next barrier was to convince an old family servant of the Tichborne family by the name of Bogle. The black retainer was either so excited at being reunited with young Roger, or had been promised some reward in maintaining the pretence, that he confirmed to Henriette that her son was indeed alive and well. Thus Orton, accompanied by his family and the faithful Bogle, set sail for England.

Seeking to avoid an early meeting with Henriette, Orton first headed for the Tichborne family seat in Hampshire, where he failed dismally to convince the locals that he was the long-lost Roger. Even the village blacksmith saw through him, saying: 'If you are Sir Roger, you've changed from a racehorse to a carthorse!' The blacksmith last remembered Roger Tichborne as a slim man with a long, pointed face, sallow complexion and straight, black hair. Yet here before him was an obvious impostor, with a florid face, greasy waved hair and weighing at least twenty-four stone.

Roger's old tutor, Henri Chatillon, also saw through Orton straight away. He could not accept that the skinny little runt he had once taught could ever have become such an obese, uncouth person. Not only that, this man was much older than Roger would have been. He bore no tattoo on his arm as Roger had, and he did not understand French, the language in which Roger had been so expertly tutored.

Orton was not to be put off. He travelled to Paris determined to convince the one person who really mattered, Henriette Tichborne herself. The reunion between mother and 'son' took place in the hotel where Orton was ensconced – with the excuse that he was too ill to travel further. The lonely Henriette, now aged, frail and confused, did not question Orton's plea that the room be darkened because of his ailments, nor that he covered his tearful face with a handkerchief. 'Oh my dear Roger, is it you?' she asked. 'Oh Mama,' cried Orton.

So desperate was Henriette to be reunited with her child that she accepted the obese butcher as her son without question. Orton did not disappoint her. He had used his time in England well, gleaning every scrap of information he could pick up about Roger and the Tichborne family. He could not physically become Roger Tichborne but he could put up a convincing charade. Even when he made the odd mistake, such as forgetting the names of schoolteachers and school friends, Henriette chose to ignore it, saying: 'He confuses everything as in a dream.' Henriette immediately made Orton an annual allowance of £1,000. His unchallenged acceptance by Henriette made him even bolder. Now was the time, he decided, to go after the full family inheritance.

The imposter returned to England to set about claiming the family estates. He read up as much as he could about the finer details of the Tichborne history and family life. He even cheekily bounced the 2-year-old twelfth baronet on his knee in a convincingly avuncular manner. And once established in Hampshire, Orton invited two old troopers of the Dragoon Guards to join the household as servants. From them, he learned all about Roger's regimental life. Finally, he agreed to sign a sworn affidavit that he was indeed Roger Charles Tichborne who had had the good fortune to be rescued from the stricken *Bella* by the Australia-bound *Osprey* which had transported him to his new life. Orton even managed to convince the Tichborne family solicitor, Robert Hopkin, of the justice of his cause.

One person he did not convince, however, was Roger's loyal friend, Vincent Gosport, who naturally asked Orton about the contents of the letter he had been given. Of course, Orton knew nothing of such a letter and Gosport realised straight away that he was an impostor. Another obvious clue to his inept deception was that he failed even to recognise his former love, Katherine Doughty.

Despite this drawback, Orton steadfastly pursued his claim that he was the true Sir Roger, heir to the Tichborne estates, and the real twelfth baronet. Progress was not as swift as he would have liked, however, and it took four years for his claim to be heard in the Chancery Division of London's High Court. During this time, two crucial witnesses on the Tichborne side had died: Henriette and family solicitor Robert Hopkin.

Orton went to great trouble and expense to assemble his evidence, one extravagant example of which was to lead to his downfall. He travelled with a lawyer to Chile to prove that he, 'Roger Tichborne', had stayed at certain villages during his time in South America. This visit could have paid off because Orton had indeed been to South America. But he was recognised there as being plain Arthur Orton, and those who remembered him also recalled that he had been there around three years before Roger Tichborne had arrived on the scene. Orton was now digging himself an even deeper hole by virtue of his South American expedition. For, apart from arousing the lawyer's suspicions, further details of Orton's own past came to light – including how, as a seaman, he had jumped ship in Chile and eventually turned up in Australia, where he had adopted the name Thomas Castro.

The hearing began on 11 May 1871. There were several witnesses who swore Orton was the man they had known either as a child or in the Dragoons. Even Roger's former governess said Orton was definitely the child she had cared for. In all, Orton called 100 witnesses to support his claim. The Tichborne family could produce only seventeen.

However, several pieces of evidence proved once and for all that Orton was not Roger Tichborne. The first came from Roger's beloved Katherine Doughty, who had since married and become Lady Katherine Radcliffe. The court was hushed as she read out the letter she had kept all those years. By contrast, the court was aghast when Orton claimed that, as young sweethearts, he had feared getting Katherine pregnant – a claim that Lady Radcliffe sniffily but convincingly denied, saying they had never been lovers. Another compelling piece of evidence was the absence of a tattoo on Orton's arm, whereas Roger was known to have had one. Then there was the mystery of how 'Sir Roger' had forgotten how to play chess or to read music. There was also the question of Orton's speech, which was certainly not that of a gentleman. As Orton himself declared afterwards: 'I would have won if only I could have kept my mouth shut!'

After a hearing, which lasted 103 days, Orton was declared an impostor and was arrested and charged with perjury. Released on bail, he spent the year in the run-up to his trial travelling around Britain giving talks at music halls, public meetings and church fetes. A subscription fund was set up to pay for his defence.

Orton eventually appeared in court to answer twenty-three charges of perjury. The trial lasted 188 days, the longest criminal hearing in British legal history. This time, a desperate but fiercely determined Orton called 300 witnesses, some from South America and Australia. The Crown called 210. As part of its case, the prosecution submitted a notebook which contained Orton's handwriting. He had written a strange motto: 'Some men has plenty money and no brains, and some men has plenty brains and no money. Surely men with plenty money and no brains were made for men with plenty brains and no money.'

The jury eventually decided that, whatever brains Orton thought he had, he deserved no more money or sympathy. They found him guilty and he was sentenced to fourteen years' imprisonment. The coarse butcher's delusions of grandeur ended in disgrace and humiliation. The measure of that ignominy was voiced by the judge who had sentenced him, who, referring to the besmirching of Lady Katherine Radcliffe's honour, said: 'No more foul or deliberate falsehood was ever heard in a court of justice.' His humiliation came as the result of medical evidence put before the court by his own defence counsel. They had argued that Orton and Tichborne were one and the same because of the miniscule size of the conman's penis. Had not Sir Roger Tichborne been nicknamed by his fellow army officers as 'Small Cock'?

The conman was released in 1884 after serving ten years of his sentence. He sold his story to a newspaper for £3,000, finally confessing that he was plain Arthur Orton but excusing himself by saying: 'The story really built itself and in that way it grew so large that I really could not get out of it.' It was a confession he was later to recant. But despite attempts to resurrect his career in public speaking, Orton discovered that people were no longer interested. He died in a humble boarding house, a broken man, on April Fools' Day: 1 April 1898. He was 64. To the end, the 'Tichborne Claimant', as he was now universally known, insisted on maintaining his false identity. The plaque on the lid of his pauper's coffin read: 'Sir Roger Charles Doughty Tichborne'.

Clifford Irving
The Billion-Dollar Storyteller

Howard Hughes was the billionaire who became famous more for his hermit-like existence than for being the planet's richest tycoon. To the world outside his darkened hotel suite, he was the 'Invisible Man', a recluse who had hidden himself away for decades. At various stages of his life a daredevil aviator, a womaniser, an oil tycoon, an industrialist and a Hollywood mogul, he was rich beyond imagination. Yet by the 1970s, the once-glamorous American magnate had chosen to live out his last days as a sickly, sad, obsessed loner in anxious isolation, hidden even from the light of day in sanitised, self-imposed imprisonment and guarded round the clock by a phalanx of sinister Mormon minders.

This increasingly bizarre existence caused him to be a figure of public fascination fuelled by intense media speculation. So one can understand the excitement of a major US publishing house when it was offered the 'authorised biography' of this bizarre billionaire, written with the cooperation of Hughes himself. It was labelled 'the publishing coup of the century' and warranted spectacular rewards for the author of the work, Clifford Irving, who successfully demanded a record advance from New York publishers McGraw-Hill. The only problem was that the 'authorised biography' was no such thing. Howard Hughes had never met Clifford Irving. He hadn't even heard of him – though he soon would.

Irving, an American expatriate living on the Mediterranean island of Ibiza, embarked on his extraordinary plot in 1970 when he read an article about Hughes in *Newsweek* magazine. Entitled 'The Case of the Invisible Billionaire', it reported that the tycoon had shut himself away from the outside world in the most extraordinary circumstances and that he was in such ill health that he no longer had proper control of his widespread business empire. Intrigued, Irving pondered how he could take advantage of the fact that the ex-playboy reputed to be the world's richest man was now a living fossil. He began to research his subject.

The last time Hughes had been interviewed had been in 1958 and since then had seemingly not been seen by or spoken to anyone outside his household. So, mused Irving, if no one could get to speak to Hughes, how then could anyone discover that a proposed biography of him was fake? Irving put the idea to an old friend, Dick Suskind, and the pair agreed to work as a team, fabricating interviews with Hughes, offering the book to a publisher and even forging Hughes's signature on papers 'agreeing' to the project.

Irving was already an expert on faking and forgery. He had won some acclaim for his book *Fake!* exposing the work of one of the most notorious art forgers of the twentieth century, Hungarian-born Elmyr de Hory (featured elsewhere in this book) who sold over a thousand of his fakes to art galleries and collectors all over the world. Irving's initial approach to New York-based McGraw-Hill was to say that he had sent a copy of *Fake!* to Hughes and had received a letter of thanks. He asked the publishers if they knew of any forthcoming books about the billionaire recluse.

Knowing something more was needed to whet McGraw-Hill's appetite, he included letters addressed to him 'in Hughes's handwriting' suggesting interest in a book about his life. Irving had practised forging the tycoon's handwriting for many hours, having seen a photograph of it accompanying the article in *Newsweek* magazine. His expertise encouraged him to pen longer and longer letters, one of them stretching to nine pages. In one, Hughes supposedly wrote: 'It would not suit me to die without having certain misconceptions about my life cleared up and without having stated the truth about my life. I would be grateful if you would let me know when and how you would wish to undertake the writing of my biography you proposed... .'

An amazing coincidence then occurred which could have ended Irving's hoax there and then. On a visit to McGraw-Hill's offices, he was told that a letter from Hughes had appeared in another publication, *Life* magazine. The publishers had taken a quick glance at it and immediately become reassured that the letters sent to Irving were indeed genuine. Irving rushed away to buy a copy of the magazine – and was astonished to see that Howard Hughes's handwriting in the reproduced letter was nothing like that he had forged in his letters. It was incredible that McGraw-Hill had not made a comparison.

By virtue of the *Life* magazine letter, however, Irving now had an even better sample of Hughes's handwriting to copy. This he did with another two letters supposedly addressed to him from the billionaire. They too were sent to McGraw-Hill. Again, no one thought to compare the second batch of Hughes letters with the first. If they had, they could not have helped but spot the differences in handwriting styles.

Irving added one extra enticement to McGraw-Hill, giving them details of phone calls he said he had received from Hughes. The publishers were hooked.

The company's vice-president Albert Leventhal offered Irving a contract giving him $100,000 on signature, $100,000 on delivery of the transcript of interviews and $300,000 for the biography manuscript. It was 7 December 1971 and McGraw-Hill announced its intention to publish the exclusive Howard Hughes biography on 27 March 1972.

Such a deal seemed to demonstrate extreme naivety on the part of such an established company. No one questioned how Irving had managed to bypass Rosemont Enterprise Inc, the company the Hughes organisation had set up to make illegal the use or reproduction by anyone but Rosemont of the name Howard Hughes. And no one queried how Irving had suddenly become a close confidant of the billionaire when he had never even mentioned his name before. McGraw-Hill, however, saw no reason to doubt Irving's sincerity. They had been the publishers of *Fake!* and now their loyal author was offering them what could possibly be the final account of Hughes's life in the words of the man himself.

Irving's book deal included several provisos: that only top executives of the company should know about the project and that there must be no attempt to contact Hughes. Only Irving had his trust. And so sensitive was the book that it should be given the code name *Senor Octavio*. Meanwhile, McGraw-Hill began capitalising on their investment. The company sold serial rights of the forthcoming biography to *Life* magazine for $250,000. The contract stated that if Hughes withdrew his authorisation of the biography at any date, that money would have to be repaid.

Word of the deal soon got out, of course. The Howard Hughes empire, in the form of his public relations firm, were thrown into confusion about the proposed book, as were a vast number of journalists. It was the first they had heard of it. All attempts to contact Hughes himself were blocked, as ever. Approaches made to his public relations company about an impending biography were met with a firm denial. But this just made journalists more convinced the book existed. The Hughes organisation always denied anything about its master.

At this point of the hoax, Irving believed that it was all a bit of fun and he could throw the plot into reverse if he so chose. He said later: 'It seemed like such an elegant act, and one from which I could withdraw at any time if I wanted. That was the great fallacy.' Irving and Dick Suskind claimed they were sucked into the hoax and then locked into the fraud.

The double-dealing duo started researching Howard Hughes in earnest. They acquired every single scrap of information they could about the man but soon realised that writing a book appearing to have had the full cooperation of their subject was a monumental task. Here fate dealt Irving a staggering piece of luck...

An old acquaintance, Stanley Meyer, contacted Irving with news of an existing, half-finished book about Hughes. It had been written by a journalist, James Phelan, in conjunction with a former employee and true confidant of Hughes, Noah Dietrich. The agent for the book had been none other than Irving's old friend Meyer.

Author Phelan and agent Meyer had parted company after the manuscript had been blocked by Hughes's mighty legal team. But that did not stop Meyer passing a copy of the uncompleted manuscript to Irving, who photocopied every page before handing it back.

Irving was now able to inform McGraw-Hill that so successful were his interviews with Hughes that the book was developing into an autobiography, written almost first hand by the subject himself. And contrary to rumours that Hughes was no longer mentally alert, he was in fact so wily that he was demanding an even bigger fee for his time and trouble. He wanted $850,000. The money, as originally agreed, was to be paid into the Zurich bank account of one H.R. Hughes. McGraw-Hill was on the point of refusing a bigger payment – until it heard a rival biography on Hughes was being prepared by another publishing house.

It was only a matter of time before Howard Hughes himself decided to take a stand over the growing number of books all claiming to have been written with his authorisation. The recluse gave his first press conference for more than fifteen years. The telephone link-up, organised between Hughes in Palm Beach, Florida, and journalists in a Los Angeles studio, was hot with denial. Hughes did not know anyone called Clifford Irving. He had not met anyone called Clifford Irving.

Irving tried one last desperate attempt to save himself. He said the voice talking to the reporters was not that of Hughes but that of an impostor. His protestations failed – and the cracks in his story began to open up when James Phelan discovered that Irving's authorised biography was stolen from his own work and produced his manuscript to prove it.

Next, McGraw-Hill officially filed a complaint with the Swiss authorities to investigate the Zurich bank account. But it was a detective agency called in by Hughes himself which discovered that 'H.R. Hughes' was in fact a woman. She called herself Helga and she made frequent visits to the bank to withdraw large amounts of money. That woman was Irving's wife Edith. Worse news was to follow for the duplicitous Mrs Irving. For not only did she suffer the shock of being exposed as a fraudster, the investigations into her husband's exploits revealed that on the occasions when he had told her he was travelling the world to set up the hoax, he had actually been in the arms of other women.

Clifford and Edith Irving and Dick Suskind appeared before two grand jury hearings on 7 February and 3 March 1972. They all confessed to their elaborate fraud. Between them, they owed more than $1,500,000 to McGraw-Hill, the taxman and their lawyers. Irving received a thirty-month jail sentence and Suskind six months. Edith Irving had twenty-two months of her two-year sentence suspended only to receive another two-year sentence in Zurich for her fraudulent banking habits.

An autobiography of Howard Hughes never did hit the bookshelves. The eccentric billionaire died on 5 April 1976. At least that was the date given. Such was the secrecy surrounding Hughes at the end of his days that no one can be sure of the circumstances of his death.

On release from jail, Irving teamed up once again with Dick Suskind. Together they wrote *Project Octavio*, the story of how they schemed to pull off the biggest publishing coup of the century.

Three decades after the death of Howard Hughes, the story was retold, this time as a movie, *The Hoax*, with Richard Gere playing the part of Clifford Irving. At the time of its release in 2007, the real Irving was persuaded to talk again about his astonishing literary stunt. The master hoaxer, by now 76, married to his sixth wife and living modestly in Aspen, Colorado, explained how he became mired in such a web of deceit:

> We thought it was just a hoax. They can't put you in jail for a hoax, can they? Especially as we still had the money to give back, as we did. I thought I'd be stopped somewhere along the line at an early stage. But then we had a run of such wonderful luck with the project that we just sank deeper and deeper into the quicksand. It's a long time ago – and I paid the price.

At the age of 87, Irving died of pancreatic cancer on 19 December 2017 at a hospice near his home in Sarasota, Florida. Excusing his fraud even to the end, he was reported as saying: 'A certain grandeur rooted itself in the scheme and I could spy a reckless and artistic splendour to the way we carried it out.'

Ronnie Biggs
Rip-Roaring Life of a Runaway Robber

On his website, Ronnie Biggs once asked: 'Is it the man or the myth that makes Ron, Ronnie, Biggsy, call him what you will, a latter-day Robin Hood or Butch Cassidy and the man who is best remembered from a gang of sixteen men who held up a mail train in 1963?' The ludicrously boastful nature of the question reveals much about the character of this legendary fugitive, a man who tried to convince everyone that he was the most glamorous crook of modern times. It also bares a quirk of human nature whereby a villain can become a popular hero if his story is tinged with a touch of glamour.

Despite being the best known of the Great Train Robbers, Biggs's reputation as a 'Mr Big' is misplaced. Indeed, not only did he play a relatively minor part in the crime, he was also a last-minute recruit to the conspiracy. What Biggs did have when he was approached by a London criminal crony, Bruce Reynolds, to join a 'big job' was the yearning to get his hands on enough money to end forever his days as a poorly paid painter and decorator with a sideline in petty thieving. In his dreams he saw a life of luxury waiting for him and his pretty wife.

The plan that was hatched, over eighteen months before the mail train hold-up in August 1963, was near perfect. It relied on information passed to Reynolds from an 'insider' that old banknotes from all the banks in Scotland were sent by night train to London to be destroyed. The money was carried in the so-called High Value Packages Coach, usually manned by four Post Office staff. That particular coach was always next but one to the diesel engine – and the one in between, containing only parcels, was never manned. Of course, not even the gang's informants could guarantee just how much money was up for grabs but already Biggs was planning a future funded with untold riches from just one night's illegal activity.

As the months went on, the train robbery gang grew in numbers and the plans became more detailed. The location for robbing the train was set at Bridego Bridge, which carries the main Scottish railway line over a lonely country road through Buckinghamshire farmland. Endless patience night after night had rewarded the robbers with the knowledge that the train was ripe for ambush from the bridge at 3am. The gang worked out that two warning lights could be switched. One, several hundred yards up the track, would cause a train to slam on its brakes; another, closer to the bridge, would bring the train to a full stop. After delegating certain members to ensure lines to trackside emergency telephones and nearby farms and cottages were cut at the crucial time, the gang was set for the big night.

That came on the evening of 7 August 1963 when Biggs and the rest of his colourful band set off from their base, Leatherslade Farm, to travel the 16 miles (26km) to Bridego Bridge. No one will ever know the full company Biggs kept that night. At least sixteen crooks put their heads together for the Great Train Robbery. Only ten were to see the inside of a jail for an extended time. No one will ever know, either, what was in Biggs's mind as he nervously joked with the likes of Bruce Reynolds, Charlie Wilson, Tommy Wisbey and Gordon Goody – all London villains with a thirst for the good life.

In place at the bridge, the gang sat and waited. At precisely 3am they saw the train approaching. Shouts of 'go, go' echoed through the air as signals were changed, phone lines cut, and coshes were taken up. Train driver Jack Mills had no reason to be suspicious when he saw a signal glowing amber for caution. He brought the train down to 30 miles per hour. Further on, he saw the red signal. Co-driver David Whitby got down from the train to telephone the signal box to find out what was going on. He called back to Jack that the first phone he tried wasn't working and that he was setting off for the next one. Before he could say any more, Whitby was manhandled by two of the gang and bundled back onto the train. Meanwhile, Mills was attacked from both sides and struck twice on the head. The gang was later to swear that physical injury was not part of the plan; that something had gone badly wrong. And no gang member has ever owned up to striking those blows, an attack from which Jack Mills never fully recovered. His health declined as a result of his ordeal and he died six and a half years later.

Unaware or uncaring that one of their members had overstepped the mark, the rest of the gang moved in swiftly. They separated the engine and two front coaches and Jack Mills was ordered to drive them closer to the bridge. With postal staff ordered to back off, the gang now methodically looted the mail coaches. Two robbers unloaded 120 of the bags while the others formed a chain, transferring them to a waiting van. In all, the gang made off with £2,631,784 – worth well over £50million today. The robbers made their way back to Leatherslade Farm where they piled up their haul in the living room. 'I remember emptying the Post Office sacks that night and seeing money flying about in front of my eyes,' Biggs recalled later.

Joy at pulling off such a massive theft was short-lived, however. Although they all disappeared to various haunts, it did not take the police long to track down the farmhouse. A broken contract by a fellow villain to sweep the place clean meant the gang's fingerprints were everywhere. Soon the Great Train Robbers' faces were on 'Wanted' posters throughout Britain. Within a year, most were behind bars. Gang members Gordon Goody, Bob Welch, Roy James, Tommy Wisbey and Jim Hussey all got thirty years, though they were released after serving twelve. Roger Cordrey was sentenced to fourteen years and served seven. Jimmy White was sentenced to eighteen years and served nine. Brian Field, a solicitor's clerk who organised the purchase of Leatherslade Farm was sentenced to twenty-five years for conspiracy, later reduced on appeal to five. Buster Edwards, who eventually gave himself up, was released after serving nine years of a fifteen-year sentence. Charlie Wilson was sentenced to thirty years, broke out of jail in 1964, but was arrested in Canada three years later. And Bruce Reynolds, reckoned to be a mastermind of the gang, was arrested in Torquay, Devon, in 1968 and sentenced to twenty-five years, of which he served ten before being released on parole.

Prospects must have looked pretty bleak, too, for Ronnie Biggs. He had stood in the dock and heard his thirty-year sentence read out. But as he sat in his prison cell, he couldn't get the thought of his secret stash of banknotes out of his mind. In July 1965, he was 'sprung' from London's Wandsworth Prison by a gang of nimble-footed, daredevil associates. Biggs scaled the wall and jumped onto the roof of a waiting furniture van. Determined no one would recognise him wherever he went, his first port of call was France where he had plastic surgery to his nose and cheekbones. He then stashed away what remained of his share of the Great Train Robbery haul (reckoned to have been £147,000) and fled to Australia.

Biggs did not splash his money about, instead working by day as carpenter and returning for quiet evenings at home in Melbourne with his wife Charmian and their three sons. They made only one major change in their lives: adopting new names. It could have been a perfect existence but for two events. The first was the death of their eldest son in a car crash, the second a tip-off that Scotland Yard were in pursuit. Charmian and Ronnie decided she and her sons would stay in Australia while he fled to Brazil. It was a decision Charmian was to regret.

With his charming smile and effervescent sense of humour, Ronnie Biggs soon became well known in the tourist bars of Rio de Janeiro. But deep down he missed his wife and family. Loneliness led him into a life of drink, drugs and women. In 1994, a reporter from a London newspaper tracked him down with the offer of writing his life story but the reporter's bosses felt obliged to tip off Scotland Yard about their exclusive subject. On 1 February 1974, Chief Superintendent Jack Slipper and a fellow police officer arrived to recapture the runaway.

Ever lucky, Biggs escaped the grasp of the law again. No one had told the London policemen that Brazil didn't have an extradition agreement with Britain – and Rio police refused to hand him over. By then, Ronnie had found a steady relationship with Brazilian girlfriend Raimunda. When she announced she was pregnant, it was more than just impending fatherhood that had Biggs overjoyed – for, by law, the father of a Brazilian child could not be deported.

Annoyingly for Biggs, he DID find himself back in prison in 1981. But it was a gang of kidnappers, not the law, who got their hands on him. Former British Army sergeant John Miller and four other men befriended him in Rio. Biggs had no reason to suspect their motives and, having split from Raimunda, he enjoyed the company. One night outside a Copacabana bar, the gang grabbed him, gagged him and stuffed him inside a sack. Biggs was smuggled out of the country, eventually arriving by yacht in the Caribbean, where Miller wanted to sell the last of the Great Train Robbers to the highest bidder. However, the yacht on which Ronnie was being held broke down and was seized by coastguards as it drifted into Barbados waters. The kidnappers escaped, leaving poor Ronnie to be thrown into the island's main jail while awaiting extradition to Britain.

Back at Scotland Yard, police teams rubbed their hands with glee. At last, they thought, Biggs's charmed life was coming to an end. It was not to be. Ronnie's best mates in Rio, Cockney John Pickston and his Brazilian wife Lia, hired top lawyer Ezra Alleyne. After three weeks of legal wrangling, the Chief Justice of Barbados Sir William Douglas ruled that the extradition treaty between the island and Britain was not valid. Biggs was walking free again, with £30,000 for the costs of his case. He strode out of the courtroom into the brilliant sunshine to be greeted by a welcoming crowd of cheering islanders. 'Champagne for everyone,' he shouted. 'The drinks are on me!'

Ronnie Biggs returned to Brazil a celebrity. His son Michael brought him additional reflected glory when he grew up to become a pop star. And every British journalist passing through Rio would call on Biggs's home for a cheery 'quote'. As he told one:

> After thirty years people still ask me how much I have left from the Great Train Robbery. Some smirk when I reply that my share had gone after only three years but it is true. A third of the money went on my escape from Wandsworth Prison to Australia, a lot was ripped off by my minders, and I gave a lot away to family and friends, which I don't regret. So don't go looking for buried treasure because there isn't any. Otherwise, why would I still be hustling 'I Met Ronnie Biggs' T-shirts to English tourists?

Thus throughout the 1980s, on any evening at a beachside bar at Copacabana, a silver-haired expatriate might be seen sipping an iced drink and reflecting on the possibility that sometimes, just sometimes, crime can be made to pay.

Biggs's success was in stark contrast to the experience of one of his partners in crime, the other famed robbery fugitive, Ronald Edwards. Nicknamed 'Buster' – the title of a movie biography starring Phil Collins – Edwards fled to Mexico after the heist but gave himself up in 1966. When freed, he ran a flower stall near London's Waterloo Station where, driven to drink by bouts of black depression, he hanged himself in a lock-up garage. From the long-distance safety of Brazil, Biggs sent his feelings of 'sorrow and affection' over his untimely end.

Edwards's death in 1994 put back on the front pages of newspapers one of the most notorious crimes in British history. But while Edwards had considered himself the most affected by the robbery – he never recovered from the nine-year prison sentence – Biggs had good reason to consider himself the luckiest. That luck held again in 1997 when, with a new criminal extradition treaty with Brazil in force, Britain again asked for Biggs to be returned. Once again, however, the Brazilian authorities declined to hand him over – this time on the grounds that the country's law did not allow for the punishment of an offender after fifteen years.

However, just months later Biggs suffered a serious stroke, the first of several, rendering him frail, housebound and barely able to speak. In 2001, after two further strokes, he decided to return to Britain. Although he anticipated a short prison term, he also expected to be hailed as a hero, saying: 'I am a sick man. My last wish is to walk into a Margate pub as an Englishman and buy a pint of bitter. I hope I live long enough to do that.'

On his return to Britain, however, he was greeted not by cheering crowds but by a police van and prison warders. The jailed robber, then aged 72, was a sorry sight, largely paralysed due to a fourth stroke. Nevertheless, he received one welcome but unexpected visitor. Raimunda, his 54-year-old ex-girlfriend, flew to England in 2002 to show her support – and despite long ago ditching the man she described as 'an unprincipled womaniser', married him behind bars at London's high-security Belmarsh Prison. Biggs was released from custody seven years later 'on compassionate grounds'. When he died in a London care home in 2013, a string of strokes had left the 84-year-old a wreck of a man, fed through a tube and unable even to mumble. But his passing was front-page news – no small recognition for a small-time felon who became the great survivor of the crime of the century

Photo Phoneys
Creating Psychic Images of the Dead

The particular specialisation of William H. Mumler was taking pictures of people who weren't there. The first exponent of so-called spirit photography, the wily American discovered the technique after an accidental double exposure revealed an ethereal second person in a photograph he had taken of himself. Realising there might be a market for such imagery, he launched a lucrative business by taking people's pictures and doctoring the negatives to add 'spirits'. In doing so, he was not only taking advantage of a period of heightened belief in spiritualism but also of those vulnerable and gullible mourners who were so desperate to see their loved ones again that they were easy targets for fraudsters.

Formerly an engraver for a Boston jewellery company, Mumler first came to public attention in the 1860s after announcing that he had not only succeeded in taking photographs of spirits but that he could repeat their capture on camera over and over again. He boasted that he was 'an instrument in the hands of the invisible host that surrounds us for disseminating this beautiful truth of spirit-communication.'

We now know, of course, that the psychic effects were achieved not only with clever double-exposure techniques but also with the use of dummies. But to believers of the time, American president Abraham Lincoln really was caught on camera flying over the head of his widow; the dead of the First World War really did look down from the Armistice Day clouds, and the face of Sir Arthur Conan Doyle did actually manifest itself in a glob of ectoplasm protruding from Mumler's nose.

It is laughable nowadays but the serious side was that so-called spirit photographers cynically preyed on the naïve, the trusting and, in most cases, the grief-stricken. Mumler charged ten dollars a time for his spirit pictures, quite a mark-up when normal portraits could be obtained for a few cents. In fact, the way Mumler worked was not much different from a normal portrait sitting. The person wanting a picture of a deceased friend or relative would simply pose in the studio. The ghostly image of their loved one would then appear on the negative and subsequent prints. Mumler, who narrowly escaped prosecution for fraud, initiated a tradition of spirit photography which continued to thrive well into the twentieth century, despite the efforts of critics – including the great illusionist Harry Houdini, who himself knew a trick or two.

One of Mumler's victims was magazine editor Moses A. Dow. He was distraught when one of his staff, a young woman called Mabel Warren, suddenly fell ill and died. In Dow's words: 'She peacefully and quietly passed to the spirit land. I will not attempt to give language to the grief which I felt at her death. She seemed like a dearly-beloved daughter, her natural father having died in her infancy.'

A week after Mabel's funeral, however, that void was filled with her spiritual presence. In a series of séances held at Dow's home using a medium – an associate of Mumler – Mabel sent messages written on slate and paper. One of these was particularly specific and ordered Dow to go to 170 West Springfield Street, Boston, where Mabel promised to show herself wearing a wreath of lilies. The address was that of Mumler's studio and, not surprisingly, Mabel made her scheduled appearance there.

In 1869, Mumler was arrested shortly after moving his highly lucrative spirit photography business from Boston to New York. He was charged with fraud, larceny and obtaining money under false pretences. The evidence produced by both the defence and prosecuting lawyers during the sensationally publicised trial matched the two attitudes towards the whole issue of spirit photography. The defence attorney argued that Mumler was using ordinary photographic methods and his success in obtaining spirit figures was not subject to his control. He stressed that the procedures had been scrutinised with no evidence of deception found and that many customers had recognised the features of departed loved ones in his pictures – even in cases where no likenesses of those people existed.

The fact that many of the spirit 'extras' in Mumler's pictures had been identified was the central feature of the defence attorney's argument. How, he asked, could identifiable spirit portraits be produced by fraudulent means? The prosecutor offered a simple explanation. He suggested that the vagueness of the spirit forms in the photographs left most of the question of identification to the imagination, and that the sitters credulously imagined they saw what they wished to see. In his words: 'Those who went to him prepared to believe, of course did believe on very slight proof.'

Though all this was perfectly true, spiritual believers felt they had a firm case, too. After all, both believers and non-believers were convinced photographs could not lie. Though the weight of public opinion was on the prosecution side, neither they nor the defence team could prove their case, and the judge dismissed all charges against Mumler through lack of evidence.

The next spirit photographer to receive widespread attention was the first to make his mark in England in the early 1870s. Frederick Hudson used drapes to obscure the spirit faces and, just like his fellow fraudulent photographers, made a very good living out of his art. He used a special camera made by a man whose normal expertise lay in manufacturing conjuring apparatus. The camera was of the old square wooden box-type but with an ingenious difference. The frame held a waxed paper positive of the desired ghostly image which, when activated by a lever, rose to place it in contact with the photographic plate, thereby leaving a ghostly imprint.

Hudson's reputation prompted a much-publicised visit from famed naturalist Alfred Russel Wallace, who went from cynic to believer when Hudson took 'portraits' of his dead mother at different ages – even though they were unlike any photographs taken during her life. Another customer, William Howitt, obtained the likeness of two deceased sons. A Dr Thomson obtained an image of a lady whom his uncle in Scotland identified as the likeness of Thomson's mother. She had died in childbirth and no picture of her remained.

One of Hudson's most regular clients was Georgiana Houghton, who drew and painted unearthly images which she claimed were produced under an 'automatic process' directed by spirits. Indeed, Miss Houghton lived her life under her own personal band of seventy archangels who not only chose her home and the wallpaper and carpets to go in it, but who even directed her feet when she went for a walk. It was no wonder she was such a follower of Hudson – for, as it transpired, she was in business with Hudson to sell reproductions of his photographs.

Édouard Buguet was another spirit photographer making his reputation – and an awful lot of money – by producing remarkable likenesses of deceased relatives of his sitters. The French fraudster's pictures not only portrayed his living subjects but the ghostly form of their dead family members. To get himself in the right mood, Buguet would put himself into a trance before taking his psychic picture. His greatest achievement was supposedly photographing the Rev Stainton Moses in Paris while sitting in a trance in London – it being later revealed that the pair had long been in collusion.

Buguet's international fame was short-lived. In 1875, a sting operation by Paris police revealed that his photographic plates had pre-exposed images on them. His trial was one of the most sensational of its day, the drama heightened when Buguet finally confessed that he had never taken a genuine spirit photograph in his life. He admitted using the technique of double exposure and to dressing up a doll or even his own assistant to play the part of a ghost. This confession rather shamed the loyal spiritualist witnesses who had supported him – including a journalist, photographic expert, musician, merchant, 'man of letters', optician, ex-professor of history and army colonel. They had largely stuck to their evidence even when confronted in the courtroom with the dummy heads, false beards, cheesecloth and other equipment with which it was claimed Buguet had achieved his photographic results. The convicted fraudster retracted his confession after the trial while languishing in prison for a year.

Despite the exposure of so many tricksters, there remained no shortage of self-proclaimed mediums who, well into the twentieth century, claimed to be able to conjure up the ghostly form of those who had passed on to the next world. One of the most celebrated was Englishman Dr d'Aute Hooper who, despite being a busy physician in Birmingham, was also credited with a wide range of psychic powers including spirit photography. He argued that the images of his ethereal visitors had to be genuine because witnesses could verify that the photographic plates he used were untouched by him at any stage of the process.

Hooper's most famous picture was that of a young spirit girl taken in 1905. The image was created when Dr Hooper had a patient staying with him to receive spiritual healing. The doctor later recounted the event...

> My patient had been out for a walk and when he came back he said: 'Doctor, I feel so queer. I feel as if there is someone with me. Will you get your camera and take a snapshot of me?' I got the camera and before I exposed the plate, I told him I saw a beautiful child with him. The gentleman himself took the plate to the darkroom and developed it. And there appeared the beautiful spirit form of a little girl with a bouquet of flowers in one hand and a roll of paper in the other. The exclamation of the gentleman was: 'Good heavens! It's my daughter who died thirty years ago.'

It is often argued that photographic fraudsters such as Mumler, Hudson, Buguet and Hooper were doing no more than easing the grief of credulous mourners. But as collector William Becker, founder of the American Museum of Photography, says:

> Spirit photography is not a victimless crime. You can see the hope on the subjects' faces. It's hope for proof that they'll soon be able to make daily contact with the dead. But it is the manipulation of photographic material and of the human psyche. The people who were producing spirit photographs had to know they were faking it.

Cynthia Payne
Bawdy House Parties of Madame Cyn

'Madame Cyn' was a brothel keeper with a difference. Her chirpiness and Cockney sense of humour meant that, far from being vilified as a vice queen, she became something of a folk legend in Britain. And when the whip-wielding madam appeared in court for the first of two infamous sex party cases, even the prosecution had to admit Cynthia Payne managed 'a well-run brothel'.

When Cynthia was arrested in 1978, she was running her sexy business from a four-bedroom house in Streatham, South London. Then aged 45, discreet and with wide experience of the pleasure game, Cynthia could count vicars, barristers, several peers and an MP amongst her regular customers. They would buy £25 worth of 'luncheon vouchers', which could then be traded in for the girls of their choice plus generous helpings of food and drink. For each voucher, the women, dubbed 'dedicated amateurs' by Cynthia, were paid a £6 fee. The atmosphere was more like a jolly swingers' party than seedy, sordid whorehouse. When the police raided 32 Ambleside Avenue they found no fewer than fifty-three men having (or waiting expectantly for) their sexual entertainment. Seventeen of them were formed into an orderly queue on the stairs – each clutching his luncheon voucher.

At her subsequent trial, police said they had watched 32 Ambleside Avenue, an ordinary house in an ordinary street, for twelve days and had counted 249 men and fifty women go in and out. One regular partygoer was Squadron Leader Robert 'Mitch' Smith, who was also Cynthia's lover. Although he had his own flat in genteel Purley, Surrey, the retired RAF officer spent most of his time at Ambleside Avenue, even giving guided tours of the neat, suburban house.

In defence, Cynthia Payne's lawyer said that her clients were so respectable that after the police raid they had simply donned their bowler hats, picked up their briefcases and had returned home as if they had spent a hard day at their offices. There had been no complaints recorded and Mrs Payne's neighbours laboured under the happy misapprehension that she was no more than an affable Streatham housewife with lots of friends. Court reports of the sexual high jinks filled pages of the popular press and were neatly encapsulated in one cartoon that showed a policeman confronting a vicar in bed with a prostitute. 'I demand to see my solicitor,' said the vicar, 'who is in the next bedroom.'

Despite Cynthia's 'tart with a heart' nature, her cheerful plea of guilty to running a brothel, and juicy tales of queues to bedrooms, the judge did not see the funny side. He sentenced Cynthia to eighteen months and a £2,000 fine for running a disorderly house. She also admitted three further counts of controlling prostitutes and was fined £650 on each charge. Cynthia was used to being penalised in her chosen career, and the indignity of being hauled before a court was not new to her. In 1965 she had appeared before Marlborough Street Magistrates Court in London and had been fined £10 for brothel-keeping. The following year, she was in the same court facing the same charge and was fined £30. Repeat appearances in 1973 and 1974 cost her £50 and £200 respectively.

Then came her highly celebrated 1980 court appearance which landed her in prison. She immediately appealed against her sentence. Despite a public outcry, backed by some members of parliament, that the prosecution had been a total waste of public money, the appeal judge refused to quash the sentence altogether. He said: 'This is conduct which is outrageous.' And of the generally middle-aged ladies involved in the luncheon voucher trade, he said: 'Some were common prostitutes, others were married women who were on the premises for the purpose of earning pin money.'

Cynthia remained in jail but her sentence was cut to six months. She served only four months of it before being released in August 1980. 'Madame Cyn' was swept away in a Rolls-Royce to sip champagne while she negotiated press contracts and publishing deals. She never expressed an ounce of regret for what she did. She said: 'I'd like to think I'll be remembered for running a nice brothel, not one of those sordid places like they have in Soho. I should have been given the OBE for what I did for the country.'

Cynthia was to hit the headlines again seven years later. Her colourful antics were turned into a movie, *Personal Services* with Julie Walters in the principal role, and it was a party held to celebrate the film that had her once more falling foul of the law. In January 1987 'Madam Cyn' put on a plain black dress and, looking more like the Queen Mother than a madam, she turned up at Inner London Crown Court to answer charges not unfamiliar to her:

> Cynthia Diane Payne, you are charged that you, being a woman, on May 30, 1986 and on diverse dates between December 1, 1985 and May 30, 1986, for the purposes of gain, exercised control, direction or influence over a prostitute, namely Leigh Richmond Rogers, in a way which showed that you were aiding and abetting the prostitution of the said Leigh Richmond Rogers.

There were nine other charges relating to other girls. Cynthia listened carefully. She had heard it all before. Only this time it would be different. This time, Cynthia was NOT admitting the charges. Defiantly, and with her permed head held high, she answered 'Not guilty' to each charge. The court was told: 'Some of you may have heard of Cynthia Payne before. If you have, so far as the prosecution are concerned, you can put out of your mind anything you may have heard of her, seen of her or read of her.' The Crown's case seemed straightforward enough. It alleged that at Cynthia's parties prostitutes were present, that invitations were selectively given out, various sexual performances took place and that so inadequate were the four bedrooms, a downstairs room and even a bed in the garden, large queues of sexually eager couples had to wait on the stairs until they became vacant.

The police had their own hero in this tale of sex for sale. He came in the rather overweight form of Police Constable Stewart Taylor, infiltrator of the parties, recipient of many lewd suggestions and witness to many sexual acts performed in Cynthia's home. PC Taylor, under the false name of Peter Tollington, had pretended to be a long-forgotten friend of Cynthia's in order to gain entry to her parties. His first introduction into Madam Cyn's social circle was at a jovial gathering in December 1985 when, according to PC Taylor, most of the men at the party were aged between 50 and 60, with one or two younger ones 'thrown in for good measure'. He then went on to describe what happened at that party and at two subsequent ones.

Keeping up the pretence of a swinging partygoer, PC Taylor allowed himself to be regularly taken into a bedroom by one of Cynthia's girls. Each time, he said, he told the girl he was impotent and preferred just to talk. Each girl was given £25 for her time. Taking his undercover duties very seriously, the policeman also watched various cabarets, such as lesbian encounters and striptease dances.

To improve his chances of getting a conviction, PC Taylor took along his 'brother-in-law Harold' (more accurately PC Jack Jones) to Cynthia's next two parties. Again, there were tales of half-naked women, men being caught literally with their pants down and propositions by a string of women. The policemen's evidence took a bizarre turn when the court heard that, to add realism, 'Harold' the undercover cop had been presented as a part-time transvestite who owned a guest house in North Wales. He attended Cynthia's parties wearing make-up and a cravat. The incriminating point they wanted to emphasise was that on all occasions, in line with other male partygoers, they each gave Cynthia £30. This was strongly denied by her.

Overseeing the whole police operation had been Sergeant David Broadwell of the Obscene Publications Branch. He told the court that at the first party, officers watched fifty-nine men and twenty-eight women come and go; at the second, forty-five men and twenty women; on the third, the night they raided Cynthia's house, thirty-five men and twenty-three women had knocked on the door. The raid came after a signal was given from inside the house. Sgt Broadwell and other officers said that throughout the property they had found men and women in various stages of undress and performing a wide range of sexual activities.

One encounter with a couple caused guffaws in court. With his voice not altering as he gave his evidence, Sgt Broadwell said: 'The girl jumped to her feet and shouted. In doing so, she knocked the male person into the bath. His trousers and underpants were around his ankles.' The good sergeant completed his evidence with the help of a large plastic sack containing whips, belts, chains, leather items and a dog collar.

When Cynthia took the witness box, she said that she simply loved giving parties. Indeed, two of the parties had been to celebrate the film about her. 'I live for my parties,' she said. 'But I don't charge anymore, although I did ask the men to bring a bottle. If they forgot, they gave me money towards restocking the drink.' Cynthia admitted she knew sex took place at her parties but said she no longer ran a brothel because it was against the law. She told the court: 'There is a free and easy atmosphere in my house and people feel uninhibited. They do what they like. Sex makes people happy.'

The defendant had the court almost awe-struck with her matter-of-fact tales of her sex slaves: men who didn't attend the parties but who turned up to clean for her stark naked in return for the odd caning. Cynthia lost her composure only once, when the death of her long-term lover Squadron Leader Smith was mentioned. He too had liked being whipped and kept his 'equipment' in a cupboard at his Purley flat. Cynthia started to cry when the court heard how her lover had lain dead on the floor for two weeks before being discovered.

Tuesday, 11 February 1987 saw a crowded court. The jury and packed public gallery had heard evidence from police, prostitutes and loyal pals of Cynthia. Now a verdict had to be reached. While the jury was out, Cynthia cheerfully signed 'Sexplicitly Yours, Cynthia Payne' autographs. When they returned, they announced that they had found her not guilty on all counts. The trial had lasted thirteen days and cost £100,000. The judge ordered that the £4,808 Cynthia had contributed towards her legal aid should be returned to her, together with costs. There was now only one thing for 54-year-old Madam Cyn to do: return home and hold a party – under the sign that hung prominently on her wall: 'My House is CLEAN Enough To Be Healthy … And DIRTY Enough To Be Happy!'

Although her wilder partying days were over, the outrageous hostess remained in the public eye. She wrote another book, the tongue-in-cheek *Entertaining at Home*, and dipped into politics by twice standing for Parliament. Campaigning to change the laws surrounding sex, she stood in a 1988 Kensington by-election for the 'Payne and Pleasure Party' and in Streatham in the 1992 General Election for the 'Rainbow Dream Ticket'. She also tried her hand at after-dinner speaking and in 2006 launched a range of 'adult' services and products.

She died aged 82 on 15 November 2015, leaving almost £1.3million in her will, mainly from the sale of her infamous Streatham home. The tributes upon her death included one from close family friend Kevin Horkin, who described her as 'a national treasure' and 'extremely colourful archetypal English eccentric' adding: 'She was a person with a very big heart who epitomised the phrase "what you saw is what you got".' But perhaps the most sexplicit analysis of the woman who made a nation laugh at its own prudery came from Cynthia herself shortly before she died: 'I suppose I'm someone who just liked to shock people,' she said. 'I used to pull my knickers down in the garden and show the neighbours my bum or dance on the shed naked. I think I've got it out of my system now.'

'Count' Victor Lustig
Cheek of the Bouncing Czech

Millionaire André Poisson arrived at the fashionable Hotel Crillon in the centre of Paris full of the joys of spring. He had every reason to feel especially good about himself because today was the day he was going to make history. Monsieur Poisson was due at the Crillon to buy the city's most famous landmark, the Eiffel Tower, and he was correct in the notion that he was about to make history – but not for the reason he expected. He was to go down in the annals of fraud as the victim of one of the most audacious hoaxes ever perpetrated.

The man Poisson was meeting that beautiful May day in 1925 was Victor Lustig – or Count Lustig as he preferred to be called. He was a trickster of the highest order, had already been arrested forty-five times and was now about to pull his most stunning stunt.

Victor Lustig was born in Hostinné, Czechoslovakia, in 1890, and found himself in Paris when his father decided he should become a student at the Sorbonne. He soon discovered that studying came a poor second to the Paris high life, financed by his skilful gambling.

The young playboy's ability to speak several languages came in useful when he later joined transatlantic liners to fleece dollars from rich American card players. He was taken under the wing of Nicky Arnstein, an expert at 'working the boats', and soon learned how to spot an easy target. The pair remained partners throughout a series of frauds in America before Lustig returned to Paris and took a room at the fashionable Hotel Crillon, overlooking the Champs-Élysées. There he met up with a new partner, fellow fraudster 'Dapper Dan' Collins. It was time too for more money-making fun – and their golden opportunity quickly presented itself.

Lustig was perusing his morning newspaper on 8 May 1925 when his eye alighted upon a report that the Eiffel Tower was in need of major repairs. The cost would be so substantial that the French government was even considering it more economic to dismantle the famous Paris landmark. The genial villains got into a heated debate. Collins thought the idea of tearing down the Eiffel

136

Tower disgraceful. Lustig argued that, surprisingly, many French people thought the monument hideously ugly. His argument was supported by the fact that the newspaper report made no mention of public protest over the government's plans.

What both men agreed on, however, was the potential for a splendid money-spinning adventure. Lustig got straight to work. He forged letterheads of the Ministère des Postes et des Télégraphes, the authority responsible for the Eiffel Tower, and discovered who were the main iron and steel stockholders and scrap metal dealers in and around Paris. He drew up a list of five suitably wealthy candidates for his confidence trick and sent each official-looking invitations from the ministère to attend a meeting at the Hotel Crillon. There they were warmly welcomed by the 'secretary to the deputy director', the dapperly attired Dan Collins. After a few minutes, the 'deputy director' himself made his impressive appearance. It was, of course, Victor Lustig.

The charismatic conman began with a warning:

> I must emphasise, gentlemen, that what I am going to tell you must be treated in the greatest confidence. Indeed, I should point out that before we sent you your invitations, each one of you was very thoroughly investigated. The nature of my news is so important, such a matter of national concern, that only the most trustworthy, the most serious, the most scrupulous businessmen in Paris are being let into my ministry's little secret.

There was a dramatic pause as Lustig waited to see what effect his words would have on the gathering. There was an expectant hush. Then he continued:

> No doubt you have read the newspaper reports. It is unnecessary for me to tell you that the Eiffel Tower, one of the more noble features of our noble city, has fallen into a serious state of disrepair. If all the work which is urgently needed is carried out, the bill will run into hundreds of thousands of francs. It is more than any of us sitting around this table could afford – and, dare I say it, more than France could afford.

After giving the five businessmen an authoritative history lesson on the Eiffel Tower, Lustig then came to the point of his meeting. Emphasising the crucial need for confidentiality to avoid 'political ramifications', he told his audience that the Eiffel Tower was being pulled down and that the resulting mountain of 7,000 tons of scrap iron was up for sale to the highest bidder. To give further credibility to his authority, Lustig then proceeded to summarise the 'official' government specifications of the tower. It was 984ft high, the base measured 142 yards in each direction and the interlaced girders were made of 12,000 sections joined together by over two and a half million rivets. The scrap dealers were spellbound.

Lustig's introductory talk was followed by the invitation to the businessmen to avail themselves of one of the 'official cars' waiting outside the hotel, and spend the afternoon viewing the Eiffel Tower. Lustig, the bogus man from the ministry, would then await the arrival of sealed bids at the Crillon Hotel. He told Poisson and the others that, because of the delicacy of the matter, the ministry could not be seen to be involved. The bids, therefore, should be addressed to 'Monsieur Dante'.

At this early stage, however, Lustig had already identified his prime 'target'. With an eye to the greedy and the gullible, he had marked down millionaire businessman André Poisson as the ideal 'purchaser' of the Eiffel Tower. Poisson was one of the provincial nouveaux riches anxious to make a name for himself in the Parisian business world and as such was judged by Lustig to be a man who would ask fewest questions in his quest to seal the deal.

Back in his office, Poisson himself was already calculating how to raise the finance needed to make the Eiffel Tower his very own. He even considered remortgaging his home. In his imagination, he foresaw newspaper headlines about himself: 'André Poisson, The Man Who Bought The Eiffel Tower.' Even when Poisson's wife said she found it peculiar that such confidential meetings were held in a hotel room, Poisson remained unsuspicious – Lustig having emphasised the fact that the ministry must be seen to have no part in such controversial dealings.

Poisson was beside himself when, a few days later, Lustig knocked on his door and told him his bid had been successful. Poisson was now required to bring a certified cheque for a quarter of his bid price to the same suite of rooms at the Crillon. Upon receipt of this, he would receive the necessary documents confirming his ownership of the Eiffel Tower and the terms on which he would be permitted to demolish it.

And so it was that Poisson found himself joyfully outside the Crillon Hotel on 20 May 1925. But as he approached the suite of rooms to meet Lustig, doubts began to creep in. He remembered his wife's suspicions about the whole business. He fingered the cheque in his pocket. It represented nearly all his assets. Lustig sensed Poisson's apprehension and knew he had to act quickly. It was already after 2pm and the banks in Paris closed at 2.30pm. That cheque had to be cashed today so that he and Collins could be on their way.

Lustig embarked on some clever play-acting. He adopted a nervous tone to explain that although he was in an important and influential position, his salary was but a pittance. He had to rely on 'commissions' to earn a proper wage. Perhaps, he hesitated, Monsieur Poisson could see his way clear to offer a commission too.

'A bribe you mean?' blurted out the astonished Poisson. Lustig merely smiled politely. Poisson relaxed. He knew all about bribes. They were a necessary evil he had come across in many a business transaction. Now he knew the man from the ministry had to be genuine. Poisson reached inside his pocket, drew out his wallet and pulled out the substantial wad of banknotes he always kept on him for such occasions. Lustig leaned over and, still smiling, helped himself to about 70,000 francs. Poisson returned his wallet to his pocket and then handed over a cheque for a further 1.2 million francs to cover the monument's sale. The two men shook hands and Poisson left, entirely satisfied with the deal – after which, Lustig raced to the bank to cash the cheque, worth about £5million in today's money.

That afternoon, Lustig and Collins boarded a train to Vienna, where they lay low. Every day they avidly read the newspapers, waiting for the storm to break – but not a word about the hoax ever appeared. Poisson had obviously decided his pride was worth more than the bundle of money he had so readily handed over. The fraudsters waited patiently for two weeks for any repercussions. Then, safe in the knowledge that the police had not been informed of their con trick, they made new plans... to sell the Eiffel Tower all over again!

And so the dodgy duo headed once again for Paris. The same deception as before was put in motion. Only this time, the victim, realising he had been fooled, went straight to the police. Lustig and Collins fled from Paris, the two confidence tricksters at last parting company.

Lustig went to America and continued duping easy targets. These included wealthy but greedy Herman Loller, to whom he sold a 'money-making machine'. Lustig even demonstrated how the machine could duplicate banknotes. A little careful preparation beforehand ensured the notes produced were genuine. So when Loller took them to a bank, their acceptance could not help but convince him the machine would make him even wealthier. Loller bought the machine from Lustig for $25,000. Amazingly, it was a year before Loller reported his worthless purchase to the police, having spent months believing that he had not properly mastered the machine. Lustig pulled the same stunt on a sheriff in Oklahoma. When the lawman tracked him down in Chicago to complain, Lustig 'made' some banknotes for him. Sadly for the sheriff, Lustig had used counterfeit money. The sheriff found himself on the wrong side of the law when he tried to use the cash and was jailed.

Lustig's cheating career continued. He even bravely attempted to swindle ruthless Mafia boss Al Capone. He took $50,000 off Capone, telling him he could double it on Wall Street. In fact, Lustig could think of no scheme to double the money, so he boldly returned to Capone, handed the $50,000 back and admitted he had failed. Lustig's feigned humiliation at having let such a great man down impressed Capone. He peeled off a wad of notes and gave them to Lustig as compensation.

The arch-conman went on to flood America with counterfeit money and was eventually arrested. He went on trial in December 1935 and was sentenced to fifteen years plus another five years for an earlier escape from a federal institution. Even Lustig could not talk his way out of infamous Alcatraz Prison. He served ten years before contracting pneumonia. Now an ailing man of 57, he was transferred to the Medical Center for Federal Prisoners in Springfield, Missouri, where he died on 9 March 1947. The death certificate did little justice to Lustig's colourful, cheating life. His occupation was recorded simply as 'Apprentice Salesman'.

Landmark Cases
Monumental Coups of the Kings of Con

A small-time American criminal named William Thompson is credited (or should that be discredited) with responsibility for the term 'conman'. Operating in New York City in the mid-1800s, the trickster would approach an affluent-looking stranger pretending they had previously met. After gaining his trust, Thompson would ask: 'Have you confidence in me to lend me your watch?' As soon as his victim obliged, he vanished.

Like so many fraudsters, Thompson used several aliases, including Samuel Thompson, James Thompson, Samuel Thomas, Samuel Powell, Samuel Williams, William Evans, Samuel Willis, William Davis, and William Brown. When finally arrested, the *New York Herald* dubbed him 'the confidence man' and the name stuck to that branch of the criminal trade. In 1849, the original 'conman' was incarcerated in Manhattan's municipal jail, known as 'The Tombs', and since then con-artists across the world have devised new ways to trick others in order to make themselves rich.

All of which goes to prove how wrong it would be to think that such an incredible scam as selling the Eiffel Tower must be unique in the annals of con-artistry. Far from it. It takes just three ingredients to create confidence tricks of similarly monumental proportions... a famous landmark, a fool gawping at it and a fraudster to dupe him.

Enter, in the latter category, a canny Scotsman named Arthur Furguson. A small-time actor, Furguson had found meagre fame, and even less fortune, touring with repertory companies in his homeland and in the North of England. He deserved better for, as an actor, he was extremely convincing. Furguson had once played the role of an American hoodwinked by a conman, and this gave him the idea for some of the most brazen confidence tricks in history. Within just a few weeks in 1925, Furguson conned three American tourists into 'buying' three of London's best-known landmarks: Big Ben, Nelson's Column and Buckingham Palace.

Nelson's Column was the first to go. Erected in honour of the great Admiral Horatio Nelson after his naval victory over the French, the column stands in London's Trafalgar Square. Also standing in the square and gazing up at the column on this particular day was a tourist from Iowa. Furguson approached him. 'The statue atop that column is of England's greatest naval hero, victor of the Battle of Trafalgar in 1805,' announced Furguson. 'It's such a pity that it is having to be dismantled to help repay Britain's war loan from the United States.'

The American was horrified. In the conversation that ensued, Furguson established that the man was not only a 'lover of fine architecture' but also extremely rich. In that case, suggested the Scot, he really ought to note that he, Arthur Furguson, was none other than the Ministry of Works official entrusted with the sad task of arranging the sale. There was already a long queue of potential buyers, warned the talkative trickster, but if there was a chance of the monument going to such a fine new home as Iowa, then he guaranteed his best efforts to see that his new-found friend would get this great edifice to Britain's former glory.

The man from Iowa was hooked. He pleaded with Furguson to let him jump the queue for Nelson's Column. Eventually, the Scot agreed to telephone his superiors there and then. Within minutes he was back with the good news that, for an immediate cheque in the sum of £6,000, he could have the monument and dismantle it as soon as he liked. The cheque was written and a receipt exchanged for it, accompanied by the name and address of the 'authorised' demolition company. The afternoon was now drawing on and the company had closed for the day. The next morning the American was on the phone to them but all he heard from the other end were howls of laughter. Tourists are always told that when in doubt, they should ask a London bobby. A bemused constable heard the American's story and led him to Scotland Yard nearby. There, at last, the penny dropped. But so did £6,000, for Furguson had already cashed the cheque and disappeared.

Arthur Furguson was now flushed with success. Within weeks, Scotland Yard again heard of his barefaced cheek when an American complained that he had bought Buckingham Palace for £2,000 yet the Royal Family would not allow him through the gates. Only days later, a third transatlantic tourist told them he had paid good money for Big Ben, the clock tower alongside the Houses of Parliament. Furguson had accepted a knockdown price of £1,000 for its purchase.

Police chiefs within the red-brick edifice of Scotland Yard were less than pleased that their neighbouring buildings were being hawked on the streets of London. Might theirs be next? However, attempts to trap the elusive Furguson came to nought. So impressed was the conman with the generosity of the American people that he had decided to emigrate there.

Once in the United States, the Scotsman's career of con-artistry continued unchecked. 'Think big' was Furguson's motto, so he offered a Texan cattle rancher a ninety-nine-year lease on a large white building in Washington. The rent was $100,000 a year, with the first year paid in advance. The Texan handed over the cash in exchange for a worthless lease on the White House!

Having attempted to dispossess the President of the United States, Furguson then attempted to do likewise to its most famous lady. In Manhattan he encountered a gullible Australian on a visit from Sydney, to whom he spun a yarn about New York Harbour's waterways being widened. The unfortunate consequence of this modernisation programme, explained Furguson, was that the Statue of Liberty was to be dismantled and sold. If relocated to the southern hemisphere, would it not look just fine re-erected on Pinchgut Island in the middle of Sydney Harbour? The unsuspecting Australian was given a guided tour of the statue, a gift to New York from the people of France. He then asked a passer-by to take a photograph of himself with the famous torch-carrying lady in the background to show the folks back home. Unfortunately for Furguson, he too was in the picture.

The Australian's next call was to his New York bank, where he made an immediate application for a loan of $100,000, the price being asked by Furguson. The bank manager was suspicious and urged his client to check with the New York Police Department. Having shown them the photograph of himself with the phoney 'city official', detectives swooped on Furguson, who ended up with a five-year jail sentence.

Upon his release in 1930, Arthur Furguson removed himself to the gentler climes of Los Angeles, where he found the pickings modest but satisfactory. He perpetrated a further string of minor confidence tricks from his luxurious new home, avoiding the interest of the Californian police until his death in 1938.

Another smooth talker who specialised in selling landmarks to unwary tourists was George Parker, one of the most audacious conmen in American history. Operating mainly in New York at the beginning of the twentieth century, he set up a fake office in the city to handle his real estate swindles. He produced impressive forged documents to prove that he was the legal owner of whatever property he was selling, which, over the years, included the Statue of Liberty, the original Madison Square Garden, the Metropolitan Museum of Art and General Grant's Tomb. When touting the latter, he posed as Grant's grandson.

Parker's favourite public landmark, however, was the Brooklyn Bridge, which he sold twice a week for years. He convinced his gullible purchasers that they could make a fortune by charging tolls for access to the roadway. More than once, police had to remove naïve buyers from the bridge as they tried to erect toll barriers. In America, his exploits gave rise to the phrase used to indicate that someone is gullible … 'And if you believe that, I have a bridge to sell you!'

Parker was thrice convicted of fraud and in 1928 was sentenced to a life term in Sing Sing Prison. He died in 1936, mourned by both prisoners and warders as a highly entertaining storyteller.

The golden age of such 'landmark' cases of con-artistry, as practised by the likes of Parker, Furguson and Victor Lustig, seem to have been between the two world wars. Indeed, one would think that after Lustig's incredible Eiffel Tower hoax, no one would ever make the same mistake again. Yet a barefaced attempt by English conman Stanley Lowe to repeat the scam shows there is no limit to what a determined fraudster will attempt.

Just after the Second World War, Lowe managed to persuade a wealthy Texan that the Eiffel Tower had been so badly damaged by the war that the city's officials had decided to sell it off, the historic monument's scrap value being a mere $40,000. The Texan fell for the story. Luckily for him, the attempted fraud was uncovered in time and Lowe was sentenced to nine months in jail.

The Eiffel Tower deception was just one in a series in Lowe's conning career. His speciality was disguise, and he regularly took on the persona of different characters. Wearing clerical gowns, Lowe once persuaded a Japanese tourist to contribute $100,000 to an 'appeal' to help restore London's historic St Paul's Cathedral. Another of Lowe's roles was as an Oscar-winning Hollywood producer called Mark Sheridan, seeking investors for a potential box-office success. On other occasions, he would become Group Captain Rivers Bogle Bland, a former RAF officer working undercover for the British government on a top-secret mission. Despite the ludicrous name he had chosen for the fictitious war hero, he still managed to convince people to part with their money.

Lowe did not always want to prise cash from people; sometimes he just enjoyed inventing stories. It was a pastime he had perfected early in life when his home was an orphanage in North London. He drifted into crime at an early age, quickly realising that you had to think on your feet to wriggle out of tricky situations. There was the time when the owner of a Mayfair apartment caught him stealing. Calmly, he explained: 'Madam, this is an emergency. I was just passing when I saw a man attempting to hurl himself from the window.' Then he coolly walked off with his pockets full of the woman's jewellery.

It was Lowe's talent for escaping justice that enabled him to lead a champagne lifestyle. He wore handmade shoes and shirts, stayed at the famous George V Hotel in Paris and went on exotic holidays. One of his plots was purposely planned to fund this lifestyle on a conveniently regular basis. Lowe talked his way into a job as a footman at Marlborough House, home of Queen Mary, where he planned to lift, steal, pinch, purloin, thieve or snaffle as much as he could lay his hands on. But his taste for high living was his downfall. One day he arrived for work wearing a designer suit and driving a brand new Jaguar car which he had just stolen. Suspicions were naturally aroused, as Lowe's lifestyle seemed a little extravagant on a weekly wage of £6.

When questioned by officers of the law, the conman told them: 'The Queen is surrounded by priceless possessions and I had nothing. It's not that I'm disloyal to our beloved Royal Family. I just decided she should be punished for her greed.' A prison sentence followed and when he was released, Lowe seemed to have lost his conman's confidence. He was never the same villain again, eventually ending his days in a humble one-room apartment. The glory days for the man who fancied himself as a modern Robin Hood – 'I want to rob the rich,' he once said – were finally over.

A more recent case of barefaced con-artistry was that of an attempt to sell London's famous Ritz Hotel. Astonishingly, trickster Anthony Lee was an unimpressive, jobless, penniless lorry driver from Yorkshire, yet persuaded interested buyers into handing over 'deposits of good faith'. Lee convinced his prime target, businessman Terry Collins, that he represented The Ritz's owners, the reclusive Barclay Brothers, who wanted to sell the Piccadilly property for £250million. Collins agreed to buy the hotel and gave Lee a £1million deposit.

In July 2020, a jury at London's Southwark Crown Court heard that Sir Frederick and Sir David Barclay had never heard of Lee and were completely unaware he was claiming to be able to sell the landmark building. Judge Stephen Robbins, sentencing Lee to five years in jail, described it as an 'elaborate and outrageous sting'. Detective Sergeant Garry Ridler who led the investigation added: 'This man is your typical fraudster. He gains the trust of people through lies and once he's got them under his control he extracts money from them.'

As a final example of how the sale of a great monument can go monumentally wrong, it is worth examining the case of what can only be described as an 'accidental con' – a classic cock-up in which the buyer ended up with nothing like the landmark he thought he had acquired.

In 1967, the City of London realised that London Bridge was slowly sinking and that it would soon need to be replaced. It agreed to sell the old bridge to Robert McCulloch, an oil man from Missouri, for £2million. However, it was only after McCulloch had paid the money that he realised he had purchased the wrong bridge. He thought he had bought the far more impressive Tower Bridge. He could do nothing about the mistake and so had the bridge taken apart and reconstructed at Lake Havasu City, Arizona. It is now the centrepiece of an English theme park complete with a mock Tudor shopping mall.

Although this was an acquisition without criminal intent, it just goes to prove that if someone wants something enough, they tend to ask too few questions. As the old adage suggests: pride in possession comes before a fall.